D1598245

systematic empiricism

David Willer
Judith Willer
University of Kansas

systematic empiricism: critique of a pseudoscience

PRENTICE-HALL, INC.
englewood cliffs, new jersey

Library of Congress Cataloging in Publication Data

Willer, David.
Systematic empiricism.
(General sociology series)
Includes bibliographical references.
1. Social sciences—Methodology—History.
I. Willer, Judith, joint author. II. Title.
H61.W555 300'.7'2 72-10555
ISBN 0-13-880351-X

Printed in the United States of America

10 9 8 7 6 5 4 3 2 1

Prentice-Hall International, Inc., London
Prentice-Hall of Australia, Pty. Ltd., Sydney
Prentice-Hall of Canada, Ltd., Toronto
Prentice-Hall of India Private Limited, New Delhi
Prentice-Hall of Japan, Inc., Tokyo

GENERAL SOCIOLOGY SERIES
Neil J. Smelser, Editor

To Jan, Bill, Ann, and Fred

contents

preface

Sociology is usually considered a social science along with anthropology, political science, economics, and psychology. All these fields do share a common methodological orientation, varying from simple description to complex statistical analysis. But it is a common fiction that the scientific method begins with careful observation and collection of facts, an error which has been compounded in the methods of the social "sciences." This book considers the difference between empiricism and science, and the extent to which conventional methods contribute to each of these types of knowledge. It examines the historical development of the methods of systematic empiricism from John Stuart Mill through R. A. Fisher, and shows that their tradition is not that of developed sciences. Empiricist social studies dominate all areas of social "science," but they do not produce either scientific or any other kind of useful knowledge.

We certainly have no monopoly on the ideas in this book, which is a product of the shared ideas of many intelligent, friendly people. We want to thank Cesar Hernandez-Cela for contributing his critique of probability in Chapter 6. We are grateful to Steve, Mel, Melvin, Richard, Frank, Dick—in fact, to a group of fine people too numerous to name—for sharing thoughts and ideas with us. We especially want to thank Susan, Bob, Roy, Jim, Doug, Len, Pat, and Cesar, who also read the manuscript for us. Last of all, we would like to thank our sweet children, who during the book's production had less of their parents' companionship than such nice people deserve.

systematic

empiricism

introduction

1 Sociology and other social "sciences" have been committed for some time to a particular methodological approach—an approach so all-pervasive that, although the commitment to it is only partially conscious, it enters unknowingly into the most diverse activities. It is a guiding force in the statement of "theory" as well as in the research process. It determines what is today sociologically legitimate and is even the basis of evaluation of historical works. It influences the manner in which we carry out our projects and simultaneously determines the meaning of sociology as it is taught and guarantees its continuance. This methodological villain is "empiricism."

"Empiricism" is often defined as an emphasis upon data collection and analysis. It is viewed as a category almost synonymous with "empirical," and those who do empirical research are sometimes called "empiricists." Since the empiricist viewpoint is so widespread, this label is frequently accurate. Sociologists who do empirical research may be "empiricists," but then they do not deserve that label any more than some who are called "theorists."

There is no necessary connection between an empiricist viewpoint and a concentration on empirical research. One may be an empiricist without ever touching data, or one may be wholly committed to empirical research without being committed to the empiricist viewpoint, as is often the case in the biological and physical sciences.

Most sociologists are familiar with the manifestations of empiricism in sociological research, particularly in survey work. Suppose that Emile Durkheim's study of suicide had been carried out in the modern empiricist spirit. Since from an empiricist point of view we never have enough facts, then the larger the sample, the more extensive the different kinds of measures and things measured, the better the study. An "exploratory" survey would, therefore, have been in order. This survey would have been concerned with finding relationships between the dependent variable suicide and certain other "variables." Data would, of course, have been gathered on religious preference, climate, race, education, occupation, age, status, place of residence, family income, marital status, voluntary group affiliation, sex, number of dependents, and so forth. The first section of the research report would have consisted of a "balanced survey" of the literature; the second would have been concerned with the populations surveyed; the third would have been concerned with the variables included and the way they were measured. The next three chapters would have presented the data analysis which would have proceeded by running everything against suicide. It might have been found that a number of chi-square tables reported associations which were significant at the .01 level. Included among these might have been differences in climate, place of residence, and sex. It might have been found, for example, that if a tendency toward group affiliation were controlled, religious differences were not significantly related, but climatic differences were not affected. Finally the content of the significant tables would have been summarized, and Durkheim would have concluded that the sociology of suicide is a new area which needs more exploration of the sort carried out in his study. This study would then have taken its place among thousands like it, none of them contributing anything to our understanding.

Of course, Durkheim did not carry out his study of suicide in the modern empiricist spirit. Durkheim's theory was not "empiricist" theory. His research was not based upon the methods of systematic empiricism. His theory did not result from empirical generalization. Although he did not succeed in developing scientific laws, at least he attempted to develop measurable theoretical constructs; and, therefore, his method was closer to the scientific method than to the methods of the empiricists. No scientific laws have been established in sociology since the rise of modern empiricism. Although Durkheim's work was not without fault, those faults did not lie in his basic orientation.

Scientific theory is concerned with concepts, terms not defined by reference to observation, which consequently enter into exact theoretical relations with one another which are often expressed mathematically. The "theoretical" empiricism practiced in sociology is characterized by the deliberate use of observationally defined empirical categories which cannot be related by any theoretical means, including mathematical connectives. Empiricist social theorizing has been general rather than abstract and therefore vague rather than exact. The purpose of theory in science is to explain, predict, and guide new research. But empiricist social theorizing consists of nothing more than generalizing, a process which summarizes what has been observed. A summary of past observations, however, cannot explain and predict, and accuracy cannot be gained from vagueness. Consider, for example, the vagueness of the statement: "It is only by virtue of internalization of institutionalized values that a genuine motivational integration of behavior in the social structure takes place, that the 'deeper' layers of motivation become harnessed to the fulfillment of role-expectations";[1] or the obscurity of terms such as *adjustive patterns,*[2] *cathectic,*[3] *appreciative,*[4] *ego-integrative,*[5] and *cognitive interests.*[6] In spite of the occasionally obscure choice of words, these terms are empirical categories, none of which is appropriate to the construction of theory. Vague termi-

[1] Talcott Parsons, *The Social System* (New York: The Free Press, 1951), p. 42.

[2] *Ibid.,* p. 48.

[3] *Ibid.,* p. 56.

[4] *Ibid.*

[5] *Ibid.*

[6] *Ibid.,* p. 57.

nology is not an indication of theoretically formulated concepts, despite its frequent use in sociology.

We have been told that the methods of sociology are scientific—or at least that the more quantitative ones are. We have been told that the lack of systematic theory, exact explanation, and precise prediction is due to the youth of social science. But social inquiry is as old as inquiry in any other subject area. We have been told that social phenomena are more complex than other kinds. But complexity is subjective, for the possession of a theory makes phenomena which once may have appeared impossibly complex seem self-explanatory. We have been told that other sciences have been more heavily funded and that their progress has been due to the sustained effort that this funding has made possible. But how many research assistants did Kepler and Galileo have? This assertion is not so much an explanation of the difficulties of progress as an expression of an economic interest in further funding. It is evident that we have been told a great number of falsehoods, the greatest of which is that empiricism is science. This falsehood, however, is the basis of the legitimization of the empiricist methods of modern sociology. It is the purpose of this book to systematically destroy that legitimization in the hope that sociologists may then be free to adopt the scientific method.

The established (and so-called "scientific") methods of sociology are not the methods of science, but those of empiricism. In fact, they even fail to meet the requirements of good empiricism. To establish these points it is first necessary to distinguish empiricism from science. For this purpose we initially present a model for a theory of knowledge which has demonstrated explanatory power, or, as the empiricists say, "validity."[7] It is therefore not open to piecemeal authoritarian (empiricist) criticism, and, since it is not an empirical generalization, it is not open to falsification. Only the development of a model of greater explanatory power can displace one of demonstrated utility. Sociologists who are satisfied with what is, and who want to continue practicing the conventional empiricist methods, must develop a valid explanation of their own

[7] See Judith Willer, *The Social Determination of Knowledge* (Englewood Cliffs, N.J.: Prentice-Hall, Inc., 1971).

if they wish to reject this interpretation of their work. This could form the beginning of scientific progress in sociology.

The false claim that conventional sociology is scientific has been foolishly accepted by the so-called radical sociologists. On the other hand, they have claimed that sociology is the handmaiden of powerful economic and political interests and that its results consist of information which the ruling classes can use against the subjugated. They believe that this is because empiricist sociology is scientific. They conclude that science is conservative and is concerned with entrenching what is. But the radical critique is misdirected. It is *empiricism* which is conservative because it is concerned with *observed* facts and thus rooted in the past. Empiricist sociologists, regardless of their value orientations, provide as a consequence of their empiricism the necessary feedback of information to powerholders for the maintenance of their domination and exploitation. This point is established later in this book. A *science* of society, because it is not dependent on what is, and because it rationally transcends existing conditions, is necessarily radical.

Scientific laws do not result from existing sociological methods; indeed, they cannot. Social science cannot result from social empiricism. Even the basis of present social empiricism is unsound. It is not useful for gathering accurate facts and generating meaningful generalizations. Its result is not only worthless as science but also worthless as empiricist knowledge. Many problems of society are due to the unequal development of the sciences and are open to solution only through the development of social science. For that purpose we need an overthrow of established methods. This book is intended as a contribution to that revolution.

empiricism and science

2 The theories and research techniques developed in some scientific fields have resulted in explanation and prediction of phenomena through the rational cumulation of laws. The basis of scientific knowledge in those fields is well established and so effective that only rarely are scientists concerned with the logical foundations of their methodology. The description of their scientific methodology has instead been left to philosophers of science, and these descriptions vary so much that those attempting to develop scientific knowledge in more unsystematic fields are likely to remain uncertain as to the nature of scientific knowledge. This has resulted in a state of confusion in those fields, which might not have come about if we had an established tradition of methods to draw upon.

After centuries of study involving an incalculable number of hours of mental labor, social phenomena still cannot be explained and predicted. The social sciencies do not have an effective, established system of scientific knowledge; thus it is not surprising that a considerable amount of social scientific endeavor has been directed toward the codification of a scientific methodology. The greater concentration on the development of methodology in the social sciences is not evidence of greater methodological sophistication, but of lack of success in constructing a workable science. We do not have a tradition of theory construction and supporting research behind us, but find ourselves instead enmeshed in a tradition of refinement of a methodology.

If science is concerned with a particular kind of knowledge, then some techniques will assist in its progress while others will head in other directions. An evaluation of the success of various techniques of attaining scientific knowledge must be preceded by an understanding of the nature of scientific knowledge and how it may differ from other types of knowledge.

One type, empirical knowledge, is gained by experience or sensation alone, and is clearly shared by man with the higher animals. Like all animals with well-developed sensory organs and a nervous system, man learns from his environment, developing expectations useful for survival. These expectations, Bertrand Russell has argued, should be admitted as knowledge.[1] The simplest human and animal behavior involves direct sensation of such fundamental needs as food and water and the immediate environment. This simple sensation alone is not knowledge; empirical knowledge involves remembering a place and developing an expectation through habit. Man, however, has an advantage over other animals in his extensive ability to communicate empirical knowledge to his fellows. It is this simplest and most fundamental type of knowledge that man shares with some other members of the animal kingdom.

In their philosophical work, the empiricists have claimed that this fundamental type of knowledge is the sole basis of thought and that man gains all knowledge through sensory experience. This school of thought is represented by the British Empiricists including John Locke, George Berkeley, and David Hume; and the British Statisticians such as Francis Galton, Karl Pearson, and R. A. Fisher; and it has more recently been found in the writings of the logical empiricists, among whom are Russell, A. J. Ayer,

[1] See Bertrand Russell, *Human Knowledge: Its Scope and Limits* (New York: Simon and Schuster, 1948), p. 429.

and Rudolf Carnap. Locke argued that men have no innate ideas because so-called truths are not universally known. They are instead learned, and often imperfectly. The learning process depends on gaining knowledge through the senses. Carrying this notion of knowledge a step further, Hume claimed that "all our ideas or more feeble perceptions are copies of our impressions or more lively ones." [2] Ideas are based on impressions, which are no more than the knowledge gained directly from sensations. A man who is devoid of sight cannot have a sensation of color or form an impression of color. Ideas are not simply reproductions of impressions; but they may be produced through various mental operations on impressions. For example, an idea of a golden mountain consists simply of combining the impressions of "gold" and "mountain"; an idea of intelligent life on Mars is formed by transposing the notion of perceived intelligent life to another planet. One event (or empirical object) may follow another contiguously in time, and this association may be observed regularly, but we cannot observe any power or force connecting them. We do not sense connections, but only the succession of events, and by the mental combination of impressions we *attribute* connection to them.

According to Hume, knowledge of causal relations is not a result of a priori reasoning—events cannot be understood in terms of pure reason. The idea of cause is no more than the result of repeated empirical observation of one object or event followed by another. No amount of pure reasoning can lead to an idea of sugar dissolving in water or an idea of falling bodies without previous experience to give these ideas meaning.

Hume defined "a cause to be *an object followed by another, and where all the objects similar to the first are followed by objects similar to the second.*" [3] Knowledge of causes is then a consequence of sensation and habit alone. If an object A_1 is sensed and followed by an object B_1 and an object A_2 (similar to A_1) is sensed and followed by an object B_2 (similar to B_1), and if this process of sensation of As and Bs continues through the sensation of an empirical association of A_n and B_n, then we come to expect

[2] David Hume, *An Enquiry Concerning Human Understanding* (Chicago: Henry Regnery Company, 1956), p. 17.

[3] *Ibid.*, p. 82.

through habit that *A* will always be followed by *B*. We say that *A caused B* on the basis of a constant conjunction of events, sensation, and habit. The observation that a particular *A* was followed by *B* may be certain because it was a consequence of direct sensation, but to say generally that *A* causes *B* is less certain than any individual observation because we cannot *observe* their connection in the future. Hume argued that nevertheless we must base our future expectations on past experience. We know that events of the present have not exactly repeated the empirical form of past events; thus our knowledge of empirical connections, causes, and effects is never certain but only probable. Although individual observations may be certain, causal connections are *attributed* to events rather than directly observed, and the general relationships drawn between similar events are uncertain. We do not perceive necessity in nature.

A general causal statement sums up similar objects (A_1, A_2, A_3, . . . A_n) in a single category *A* (the cause) defined ostensively by a set of similar observed characteristics and connected with another similarly defined category *B* (the effect). Such a causal statement has its whole basis in experience and is often called an empirical generalization. Hume stated that causal statements are formed through habit or constant empirical association or, in more modern terms, through induction by enumeration.

Hume's thinking implies both a method of investigation and a kind of explanation. To determine causes we formulate categories (*A*, *B*, and so on) of objects and events on the basis of respective similarities. The relationship between *A* and *B* is then observed either as it naturally occurs or through manipulation, and the continued presence (or absence) of the sequence is noted. Finally, having enumerated a large enough number of cases, we conclude (through habit) that *A* is (or is not) constantly conjoined in experience with *B* and consequently that *A* causes *B*. After completing such an investigation, we may expect that in future cases when we observe an object or event which may be counted as an *A* and another which we may call a *B*, we can explain this association causally—this *A* caused this *B*. Our justification for this new application, according to Hume, is that we expect this new case to be not unlike our previous experience.

Modern empiricists have been critical of Hume's approach because they recognize that general knowledge in science is certain rather than merely probable. These scholars, logical empiricists and logical positivists, attribute this certainty to the rigorous connection available through the use of the rules of formal logic. A statement such as "All swans are white" is merely an unsure empirical generalization which is tested again and again each time a new observation of swans is made; but if it is put in the form "If all swans are white, and I observe a swan, then this observed swan is white," it is contextually and thus necessarily true no matter how often a swan is observed. Modern empiricists would add this type of logical necessity to Hume's empiricism in order to gain the degree of certainty they observe in scientific relationships. In sociology we might say, "If all societies have stratification, and if this is a society, then this society has stratification." This statement is also necessarily true; however, such a statement is not an expression of a relationship but is actually no more than a definition of the term *society*. It gains its necessity by excluding all social collectivities which do not have stratification from the definition of a society. It arrives at necessity through empirical exclusion and strategically eliminates observables that do not conform. While it does remove the uncertainty of empirical–causal statements, it does so by eliminating their causal connection, their basis for prediction. In the substitution of empirical–definitional connection for empirical–causal connection, predictability and explanation cannot even be attempted. We are left with logical certainty without empirical utility. Our statement is true because it allows us to ignore observations that do not fit the definition. "Analytic induction" uses this approach and leads to such statements of logical necessity but not to the type of necessity of prediction and explanation that characterizes scientific laws.

Western philosophers have frequently opposed empiricism with rationalism. The difference is between an approach to knowledge in which only observation may lead to truth and one in which only true rationality (or inner reflection about ideas or concepts) may lead to truth. Russell argued that René Descartes' statement "I think, therefore I am," amounts to no more than saying, "I think, therefore I think I am," an assertion which seems ridiculously obvious. Nevertheless it does demonstrate the basis of rational knowledge in the determinative connection of ideas through reason. "I think, therefore I think" is true because of its form—an identity formed by reason.

Following in the rationalist tradition, Immanuel Kant believed that the laws of mathematics and physics were arrived at through the employment of determinative mental operations. Laws are not discovered through experience and observation but result from the operation of human reasoning. Kant argued that, although knowledge is in part derived from experience, this experience is ordered by our minds:

> "It is true that space and time contain what is manifold in pure intuition *a priori,* but they belong also to the conditions of the receptivity of our mind under which alone it can receive representations of objects and which therefore must affect the concepts of them also. The spontaneity of our thought requires that what is manifold in the pure intuition should first be in a certain way examined, received, and connected, in order to produce a knowledge of it."[4]

Rationalists would maintain that the statement $x = vt$ (distance equals velocity multiplied by time) is a product of the operation of reason. Although this statement orders facts, it is not the result of observation and habit; $x = vt$ is not an empiricist probability but a necessity resulting from a definition of velocity as equivalent to distance divided by time. Here the meaning of velocity is given by its formal relationship to distance and time and not by the observation of empirical association or cause and effect. This law is not an empirical generalization of the form "all *A* is *B*" or "*B* is caused by *A*" but a formal relationship of terms in which their meaning derives from reason. Rationalists would extend this claim to cover the other laws of physics (such as the law of levers, $ml = m'l'$, a self-evident identity) and in fact to all scientific laws. This agrees with Albert Einstein's observation that the theories and laws of science "are free inventions of the human intellect."[5]

[4] Immanuel Kant, *Critique of Pure Reason*, tr. F. Max Muller (Garden City, N.Y.: Doubleday & Company, Inc., 1966), p. 60.

[5] Albert Einstein, *Essays in Science* (New York: Philosophical Library, 1934), p. 15.

Scientific laws are formed by concepts which stand for ideas rather than by empirical categories which stand for impressions; such laws are not empirically definable. These concepts are related by rational, nonobservational, connectives such as equals signs. Rationalism (as might be expected) is reasonable, but there remains the problem of explaining how rationalistic ideas can be empirically relevant unless one simply has faith that the ordering processes of the mind will always work, a notion similar to the empiricist faith that the world is ordered.

Rationalist thought in the Western tradition has not been limited to the theoretical component of science, but it has also been evident in theology where the question of empirical relevance is not a problem simply because theology makes no empirical connections. Theology is concerned with concepts (such as God), which cannot be defined by empirical observations. Perhaps because of the crucial place of rationalism in religion, historical conflicts between religion and science have often been viewed as conflicts between rationalism and empiricism, an opposition of reason and fact. The controversy between religion and science over such questions as the location of the planet Earth in the center of a universe created by God versus its position as merely one of a set of planets rotating around the sun, or man as the special creation of God versus man as the result of centuries of evolution has been seen as a contrast of faith and reason with fact and observation. Some schools of philosophy still hold rational and empirical knowledge to be irreconcilable.

While empiricism and rationalism have dominated Western philosophy, the type of knowledge sought by some philosophers of the East rests on a different kind of thinking. Eastern knowledge has been gained through abstraction from the empirical to the pure idea, such as nirvana. Such thinking which bridges the empirical and the rational will be termed *abstractive;* it may be clarified for Western thinkers by reference to Plato's postulation of a world of forms in which the diversified objects of experience are reflected in a pure idea, or form, which those objects resemble but never achieve. We can conceive of a perfect equilateral triangle and a square as objects of a conceptual world removed from the world of experience in which the sides of a triangle or a square are never perfectly equal. More concrete empirical objects, such as tables and chairs, might also have perfect types.

A more modern example of abstractive thought may be found in the work of Max Weber, who proposed the use of ideal types as a crucial part of his sociological methodology. According to Weber, the ideal type "is formed by a one-sided *accentuation* of one or more points of view and by the synthesis of a great many diffuse, discrete, more or less present and occasionally absent *concrete individual* phenomena, which are arranged according to those one-sidedly emphasized viewpoints into a unified *analytic* construct. In its conceptual purity, this mental construct cannot be found anywhere in reality." [6] In the historical context of German idealism, Weber proposed that Plato's utopias be used to achieve conceptual clarity in science.

The Meaning of Methodology

Methodology is the scientific study of the means of obtaining human knowledge. Defined in this way, methodology may be differentiated from the philosophy of science and the construction of techniques, two concerns with which it is often confused. The philosophy of science has been both descriptive and speculative. When primarily descriptive, it is indistinguishable from the history of science. When speculative, it has often been an ideological pursuit wherein a fixed conception of science is the basis for interpretation of what science is. Technique construction is considerably narrower than methodology and is usually pursued for the practical aim of acquiring knowledge. For example, techniques such as contemplation may be effective means for acquiring mystical or religious knowledge, and the religious or the mystical person might be expected to refine the technique of contemplation. On the other hand, the development of techniques of contemplation may be of no utility to the scientist who employs different techniques of acquiring knowledge. Much of what has been called methodology in sociology is no more than the development of techniques of

[6] Max Weber, *The Methodology of the Social Sciences,* tr. E. A. Shils and Henry A. Finch (Glencoe, Ill.: The Free Press, 1949), p. 90.

observation. *When systems of knowledge differ in type, those techniques which are effective for acquiring one type of knowledge are not necessarily effective for others.*

Methodology as the scientific study of human knowledge requires a theory of knowledge from which determinative implications can be drawn. A model provides a basis for determinative explanation, but it is not absolute and may be altered or displaced by others that have different structures and provide more effective explanations. The acceptance of a particular model is solely for practical purposes—that is, for its isomorphism with empirical structures and thus its effectiveness in providing an explanation for them.

For these reasons, methodology is not a normative concern. As Durkheim pointed out, a norm is characterized by its power of *social* constraint in the form of sanctions. Constraint of this sort must not be confused with other consequences of behavior. When a theory of knowledge implies that a particular technique is either effective or ineffective as a means for acquiring a type of knowledge, this implication is not a rule one must follow to avoid a sanction but a statement concerning the necessary consequences of behavior. A theory, therefore, dictates an action only in the sense that it is a means for calculating the utility of that action in terms of the end desired.

Types of Thought

In the theory of knowledge presented here, the three types of thought—empirical, rational, and abstractive—are considered basic. Each involves a different type of connection in thinking. Empirical thought consists of the connection of observation to observation; rational thought connects idea with idea; and abstractive thought connects observation with idea.[7] Empirical connection is often stated in terms of association and cause, rational connection may use logic or mathematics, and abstractive connection is often char-

[7] The following discussion is based on a theory of knowledge developed in chapter 3 of Judith Willer, *The Social Determination of Knowledge* (Englewood Cliffs, N.J.: Prentice-Hall, Inc., 1971).

acterized by selective definition. These three types of thought are represented in Figure 1. There thought connection is made at two levels, the observational and the theoretical. The terms represented by the small circles at the observational level are referred to as observational terms or empirical categories, and the circles at the theoretical level represent ideas or concepts. Thought connections reserved to the observational level are empirical, connections made only at the theoretical level are rational, and connections which cross the two levels are abstractive.

Although empirical thought, as described here, closely conforms to what Hume meant by empirical thinking, abstraction is given a particular meaning quite different from the everyday meaning which simply refers to a general term. An abstraction may be specific in that a conceptual meaning of an idea may be less ambiguous and more exact than the observational term with which it is connected, which may be defined or designated by an unspecified number of empirically observable characteristics. Similarly, the meaning of rationality has specific implications here. It is narrower than the meaning employed in everyday usage and in sociological literature. We do not mean, for example, that a rational thought connection necessarily shows good sense or intelligence and is opposed by irrationality which indicates an inability to think a thought through to a meaningful conclusion. Here a rational connection is one of a specific type (connecting an idea to an idea), and, while some thought connections are not rational, they are not necessarily irrational but are merely of a different type (empirical or abstractive). An empirical thought connection is nonrational, but it is not irrational and may be better described as sensible, for it implies the direct empirical connection of sense data. Thus, a sensible con-

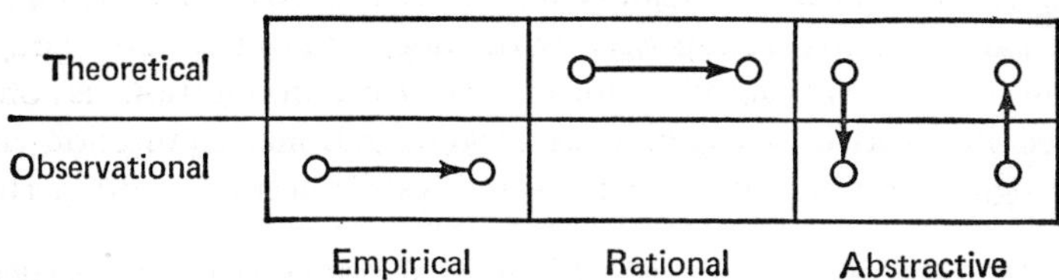

FIGURE 1. Three types of thought

nection is not rational, and a rational connection is not sensible in that it is not empirical.

The specific theoretical meaning of rationality is also at variance with its meaning in the study of formal organizations derived from Weber's use of *Wertrational* and *Zweckrational,* which have been translated as value rational and purposive rational, respectively. Value rational, when it refers to connection of ideas, is roughly equivalent to the conception of rationality used here; but purposive rationality is quite different and refers to a kind of empirical connection.

Systems of Knowledge

Systems of knowledge may be limited to only one type of thought connection, such as pure mathematics which uses rational connection alone, or they may use combinations of the types. Mathematics, in that it is an isolated system of conceptual entities and their relationships, is theoretical knowledge with no empirical referent. Abstractive thought is typically associated with either empirical or rational thought in specific knowledge systems because it has neither empirical practicality nor rational calculability if used alone; it does not provide a basis for projection in thinking. Empirical connection, on the other hand, is often used alone in the process of daily activities and may make up a complete system of knowledge, an integrated set of perceptions of the world, an approach which we call empiricism.

Empiricism (or an empiricist system of knowledge) may be found in diverse social circumstances and may be very different in content in those various contexts. Its use may vary from primitive magic to modern technology. According to James G. Frazer, "The offering made by the Brahman in the morning is supposed to produce the sun, and we are told that 'assuredly it would not rise, were he not to make that offering.' "[8] This statement involves the connec-

[8] James George Frazer, *The Golden Bough: A Study in Magic and Religion* (New York: The Macmillan Company, 1958), p. 91.

tion of observable to observable—the Brahman's offering and the rising of the sun. In Hume's terms, we might note that an observable object (the offering) is followed by another object (the appearance of the sun) and that, for all cases observed, the set of objects similar to the first was always followed by the set of objects similar to the second. From Hume's point of view, the Brahman's offering may be said to have *caused* the sun to rise. Similar examples may be found in Frazer's work, including the notion that some people have the power to avert storms and that some objects may cause fertility. These instances, typically described as cases of magical belief (and often thought of as supernatural), are concerned with the connection of observable terms. Even those who sell the fertility objects would not claim that success always follows. This is consistently an empiricist point of view. As Russell pointed out, acorns may cause oaks, but pigs may eat the acorns. Although acorns are not always followed by oaks, we still speak of acorns as causing oaks. In an empiricist world of multiple causation, the empiricist should not expect to have notions of invariant connection. Causality does not have such implications.

Today, however, we do not accept many of the empirical connections made in earlier (or more primitive) cultures. We label them "magic" and describe them as false or spurious. We believe our empirical thought connections but disbelieve theirs. In short, the differentiation of magic from other forms of empiricism is no more than ethnocentrism; our ideas are sensible, but theirs are not.

Modern empiricism is logically identical to magic, but our greater powers of observation, measurement, and manipulation often mean that our empiricism is more effective. Through agricultural technology, we have developed plants that yield larger harvests; and in many of our endeavors our empiricism has become highly systematized, leading to more refined observational techniques. The development of science for empirical use has increased the powers of empiricism; but as long as a scientific knowledge system does not displace empiricism, the empiricist logic remains identical to magic.

The empiricist conception of cause involves the notion that one object has the *power* to cause another. Power is simply the successful initiation of a causal connection. The first billiard ball, because of its motion, had the power to make the second ball roll. The first caused the second. Empiricist power is the ability to make empirical connection, and it is inherent in objects. In certain societies, individuals who are successful in gaining their ends (which necessarily entails their making empirical connections) are referred to as *powerful.* Power is both the explanation of their success and the measure of it. Class and status rankings in modern societies are clearly concerned with empiricist power, the differential ability of individuals to gain their ends consistently.

Existing forms of social organization can be interpreted from the point of view of empiricism and empirical power. Trial and error methods may lead to effective results, and when they do, procedures are routinized according to the actions carried out. The connection of routines and subroutines in a single organizational structure constitutes a division of labor. The assurance that routines will be carried out is based on the draining of power from those who do the routines to their supervisors. Organizational structures with large numbers of powerless members are usually called totalitarian. The increase of effectiveness of control by power holders leads, therefore, necessarily to totalitarian structures.

Figure 2 represents the logical form of empiricism and two other systems of knowledge: religion and mysticism. Empiricism or magic consists of empirical thought alone; religion, in contrast, does not connect observables to observables. In religion, power does not reside in empirical objects but has been removed to the theoretical level to a nonobservable concept such as God or gods. Because empirical events are not directly connected, they must be explained

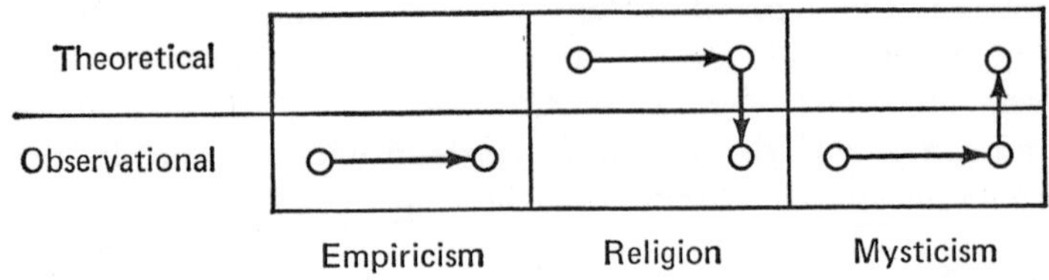

FIGURE 2. The logical forms of empiricism, religion, and mysticism

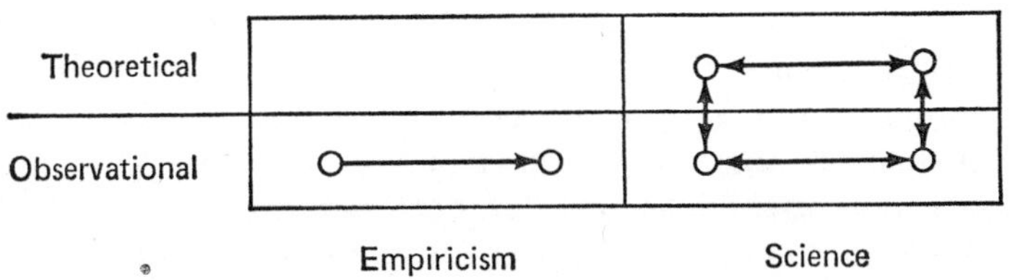

FIGURE 3. Difference in logical form between empirical and scientific knowledge

as the consequence of the action of such an abstract power source. The attempt to understand God—theology—consists of the connection of nonobservable concept to nonobservable concept and thus is a system limited to the theoretical level. This system is not subject to empirical refutation and, therefore, it becomes absolute but at the expense of empirical content. The ethical content of religion is abstractive, simply connecting idealized concepts with observable conditions.

In mysticism, abstraction plays the most important role in the thought processes and consists of the search for a single ideal. The empirical component of mysticism involves familiarity with the empirical surroundings simply in order that the mystic has empirical knowledge of those facets of experience which must be discarded in the search for the ideal mystical state. Power consists of mentally abstracting oneself from the empirical, and is thus nonempirical. Neither mysticism nor religion offers an explanation for the association of events. Mysticism ignores the problem, and religion attributes every occurrence to a nonobservable concept of God. Only empiricism and science are capable of offering such an explanation.

Science and empiricism have frequently been confused because they both offer explanations of empirical events which use observation in contrast with other types of knowledge systems. Although both science and empiricism are concerned with empirical connection, their similarity ends at that point. The logical form of science is much more complex. The difference between these two knowledge systems is represented in Figure 3.

Science, like empiricism, is concerned with empirical connection; and like mathematics and theology, it is concerned with rational connection. But it is through the abstractive connection of theoretical concepts with observations that those concepts gain empirical meaning. Scientific knowledge does not consist of successful rational connection alone, nor does it consist of successful empirical connection alone; instead, it makes rational connections which correspond to observational connections. This is the isomorphism of theory and observation, a structural similarity between the theoretical and observational levels; and power in a scientific system of knowledge consists of the establishment of this isomorphism.

In spite of the common confusion of science and empiricism, the only thing they have in common is the explanation of observable events. However, their means to this end are completely different. Science uses laws and theories, which have been interpreted by abstractive connection to empirical events for at least some of their relevant scope. Empiricism is concerned with empirical generalizations or causal connections of observational terms through the observation of empirical association. Explanation through the use of laws is very different from explanation in terms of empirical generalization. One might, for example, explain the hole in an automobile radiator on a cold day in terms of the ice observed within it. We know of other cases in which cars left out overnight, whose owners have neglected to add antifreeze, have had broken radiators resulting from the ice formed in the cold weather; therefore, we may make the empirical generalization that cold (or freezing) weather is associated with broken radiators in the absence of antifreeze. It was cold last night, your radiator was unprotected, and therefore it broke. This explanation uses an empirical connection in which all terms (radiator, cold, broken) are observational. The connection is made as a consequence of the experience of repeated observations. Explanation consists of making a general causal statement about radiators and cold and applying it to a particular case. This sort of explanation is typical of those we offer for day-to-day occurrences and is adequate for such purposes. It is based simply on observation and habit.

A scientific explanation, on the other hand, employs not general causal statements, but determinative laws. We might, for example, begin with the idea that under conditions of perfect elasticity, stress is equal to strain. We would then attempt to determine a value for the limit of elasticity for the radiator and possibly carry out an experiment with a similar radiator to determine that limit by measuring the amount of force applied before the radiator breaks. By measuring the air temperature and the temperature of the water on the cold night in question, we may determine the point at which the water would freeze and produce enough ice to apply the stress that would bring the radiator to its strain limit. A stress greater than the strain limit will result in a broken radiator.

In this explanation we are using a law, a statement of identity, in which stress is equal to strain and both terms are measured by force. This law holds under the conditions stated (within the limits of perfect elasticity of the object) and the concept "elasticity" is abstractively related to the observational term "object." The explanatory utility of the stress–strain law has thus been demonstrated, but we have not tested its empirical truth in the sense that we might test the causal connection between cold and radiators by simply submitting another radiator to the cold. The law was used within specified conditions of application; when interpreted empirically this means simply that stress is equal to strain within the limits of elasticity or that stress is equal to strain unless it isn't! The purpose of the use of the law was (1) to derive a measure for the strain limit by applying stress, and (2) to compare the calculated stress at the time of breakage with that limit. Considering that the value of the strain limit was determined from a calculation of stress, it is difficult to imagine how the law could be proven false in such an application. Clearly the "testing" of a law is different from the testing of a causal connection.

We seldom use scientific explanation as a basis for determining the course of our daily behavior; it is more complicated in its application than simple causal explanation. Since our daily activities seldom require such exactitude in the type of knowledge employed, causal explanation is an adequate basis for action. Most of our behavior is therefore conditioned by an empiricist system of knowledge.

Scientific knowledge is more precise than empiricist knowledge but not because the means of measurement in science are more precise, for any measurement used in science could also be used in empiricism. The greater precision of scientific knowledge comes instead from the determinativeness of its rational connections, their abstractive connection to empirical events under specified conditions, and the consequent precision of their empirical interpretation. The exact calculations made in scientific explanation are a result of the exactness of its connections. Causal connections and other empirical associations do not permit such calculations. The statement that cold caused the radiator to break cannot be reduced to the statement that cold is equal to a broken radiator. Our empiricist connections are by inference rather than calculation. Certainly we can measure the temperature exactly and make the statement that the colder it gets the more likely it is that radiators will break (and we can possibly even determine a "probability" distribution based on temperature variation); but this does not result in an exact calculated value of a limit. The empirical association, because it is concerned with the general behavior of radiators, is merely probable; while, in fact, a particular radiator either will break or it will not. The explanation should give that type of precision. While a scientific law can point to a measurable condition under which breaking will occur, the empiricist can only claim that the radiator is likely or unlikely to break. It will not, as an observational fact, break with a probability of .8, but it will definitely break or not break. When empiricism forces us to make statements about the likelihood of events (the most systematic type of calculation that can be made with this type of knowledge), there is some question about whether such statements have any meaning at all for particular occurrences; but if they do, they are false.

Science and empiricism differ in the way they transcend particulars in individual cases. Empiricism transcends particulars by generalization, in which a name is applied to a set of *similar* objects, forming an empirical category defined by those objects included within it (car, house, tree, gold, and so forth), and then is related to another, similarly defined, empirical category through an observational process. Rules of thumb (such as the use of correlations or probability estimates or simply the succession of repeated events described by Hume) are used to establish the conditions under which observations may be empirically related.

Science, however, transcends particulars by abstraction, a process very different from generalization. Scientific laws are not generalizations; they are not concerned with similarities, and they explain observational phenomena which are not at all similar in appearance by the use of abstracted concepts whose meaning is not derived from the similar appearance of the empirical phenomena to which they are related but from their relationship to other concepts in theory. A billiard ball does not look like a rocket, but both may be abstractly connected with the concepts of the same laws of motion. Abstract concepts are not general; they do not sum up past cases, but they are arrived at by a mental process of selection. In this process one asks how observations of phenomena can be conceptualized so that they may be related determinatively to other concepts. While empirical generality gradually builds up as more and more cases are observed, abstraction defines a potentially infinite universe at once to provide the conceptual framework for a theoretical statement. Theoretical concepts are rationally connected and their empirical interpretation is not like the sequentiality implicit in a causal connection between empirical categories. We may use the relationship, $x = vt$, but we do not observe distance to find out if it will be followed by velocity multiplied by time. Abstraction in science moves from the observational level to the theoretical and back to the observational level. Thus, there is a continual abstractive process which forms a dialectic through which theoretical statements may be modified or expanded to sharpen their explanatory power and increase their scope of application. Generalizations, however, are either true or false and must be either rejected if a contrary case is found or stated as a probability, which has the drawback that it is incapable of explaining particular cases. Abstraction and generalization are similar neither in logic nor practice.

Generalizations are summarizing statements based on two or more observations of similarities. The terms of such statements as "All societies are stratified" and "The correlation of status and voting propensity was .53" gain their meaning through the observations made. Such terms—"observables"—are defined either ostensively or operationally. Abstraction, however, is a logical procedure for connecting theoretical (mathematically or logically constructed) statements with observable phenomena through nonobservable constructs or "models." When scientific theories are used for prediction and explanation, models generated from the theories are structural representations of the relationships dictated by the theories. Conversely, the creation of a useful theory requires the abstraction of a pure structural model from the diverse material of observation. In other words, abstraction does not proceed by summarizing observations, but by generating a nonobservational structure which deliberately does not summarize. The abstractive process, because it links theory to observation, is never complete without both. Theory, on the other hand, can be applied only through abstraction.

A theory is a constructed relational statement consisting of nonobservable concepts connected to other nonobservable concepts. Concepts are defined not in terms of observations but by their relationship to each other. Although it may be meaningful to state "There is a cow," the statement "There is a force" is senseless because force is not an observable. Conversely, the statement "Force is equal to mass times acceleration" is meaningful because nonobservable concepts can be related through mathematical connectives; but the statement "Cow equals four legs" is meaningless because observational terms cannot be so related. In other words, the truth of scientific theories is not an empirical truth based on observation; it is a consequence of form, the relationship of nonobservables.

The confusion of scientific laws with universal empirical generalizations may be traced to Kant's insistence that all statements must be either analytic or synthetic. Scientific laws superficially appear to be analytic in that they form a rational definitional system, but they may also appear to be synthetic in that their application results in the relating of observations. Because all statements must be either analytic or synthetic and because scientific laws appear to have some of the characteristics of both, this viewpoint leads to a confusion of laws with generalizations. This dilemma may be resolved by defining terms as either observables or nonobservables, leading mathematically to three possible types of combinations of terms in thought. When observables are defined by other observables, the result is synthetic (empirical thinking) and is the basis for empirical generalization. When nonobservables are defined by other nonobservables, the result is analytic and is the type of thought used in scientific laws and theories. But a third type of thought connection is possible—the relation of observables to nonobservables—and this process is abstractive. Therefore, if theory (composed of nonobservables) is to be connected to observables, it must be done by abstraction.

Suppose, for example, we wish to explain the movement of a basketball down a hill. We may imagine a model of a plane *A* inclined from the horizontal at an angle and connected to a plane at the horizontal as in Figure 4. On plane *A* is a sphere *S* at point P_1 at time T_1 to which we attribute a mass *M*. By elementary physical laws, the time of motion (T_1 to T_2) from P_1 to another point P_2 on the horizontal plane may be calculated. Thinking of the sphere rolling down one plane and across the other follows from the use of the laws. In this sense, the model is animated through the laws. All the terms in the explanation at this point are conceptual, that is, nonobservables.

Given that a basketball is reasonably spherical, that a hill has a reasonably flat surface, and that the weight of the ball and distances correspond to the quantities of the model, the time required for the ball to roll a given distance can be experimentally determined. When that time corresponds to that calculated in the model, the

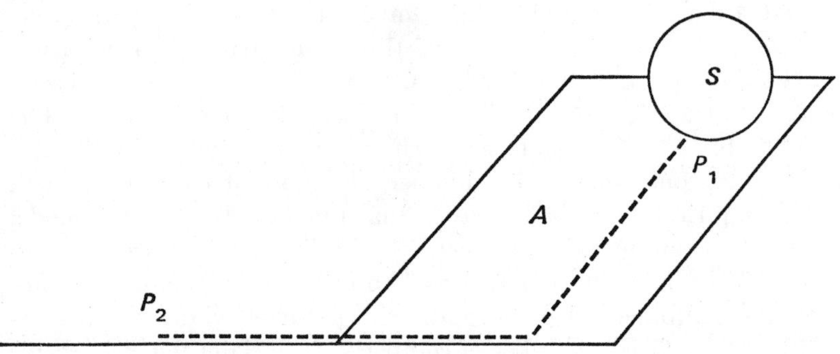

FIGURE 4. Illustration of a geometric model

motion has been explained; and, if the calculation was done before the experiment, it was predicted.

Abstraction is therefore a matter of establishing an isomorphism between theoretical nonobservables and empirical observables. Whereas generalization is confounded by the problem of figuring out "How similar is similar?" because of the unlimited number of observable points of similarity, abstraction has no such problem. In abstraction, empirical circumstances may either be manipulated in the laboratory or elsewhere to approximate the model in all relevant respects, or they may be fixed (the hill might be exceedingly bumpy and the ball might be a football) while the model is varied so that it is isomorphic to them. Often it is possible to make an empirical case as similar as one wishes to a fixed model. On the other hand, it may be possible to construct a model similar in all important respects to the empirical case. The more similar the model and the empirical case are in all the respects covered by the theoretical statement, the better the theory will explain or predict. The point of indifference is reached when the error in prediction is within the limits of measurement error.

As long as one has a theory and a model for it, empirical cases can be explained by it with a high degree of exactness, whether or not the scientist has the physical power to control them. Thus, there is no problem of "how similar" in abstractive connection, no problem of what to "control" next.

Whereas generalization involves the unanswerable problem that there are a potentially infinite number of points of comparison between any two empirical events, this is not true when empirical cases are abstractively related to theory. The model—a nonobservable, abstractive tool—is limited in descriptive characteristics. The model has a denumerable set of characteristics (limited by the theory) and consequently the number of points of comparison with any empirical event is limited to that number. Because the model is a deliberate mental construct, its descriptive points are necessarily limited by that construction. Abstraction, therefore, does not have the problem of determining the point at which one has exhausted a sufficient number of comparisons to claim that two events are similar. Abstraction, indeed, is not a process of comparing empirical events at all.

Prediction and explanation in science are, therefore, the result of calculation of possible values through the use of mental constructs, which are a product of the imagination rather than of the senses. They are not prognostications based on yesterday's knowledge (generalizations) or statements based on the physical power to exert control over immediate events. Both science and empiricism are intended to explain or predict empirical particulars, the former by mental arrangement and the latter, if it is to be successful, by direct influence. Both, in other words, are intended to be useful to individuals in explaining or managing their surroundings. Science, however, may be used for managing because it *explains first,* because it sets up mental constructions in terms we may understand. Empiricism, on the other hand, explains *only if it manages.* In other words, if we do not have the physical power to force the circumstances to conform to our expectations, then we have no reason to trust our expectations. If we cannot arrange events so that "fifty percent of lower-class whites fail to complete high school," we cannot expect our "relationship" to stand the test of experience.

A theory, although it does not result from a collection or generalization of experiences, may be applied to an unlimited set of cases. Because the number of models that may be generated from a theory is limited only by one's ability to generate them, theories, no matter how narrow their meaning, are characterized by "nonlimited scope" in the same sense that all lines (regardless of length) have an infinity of points. It is mathematically impossible to add an infinity of empirical cases into a generalization, but a mental construct may subsume a possible infinity of cases by abstraction.

The models which can be generated from a single theory may be very dissimilar. Consider the great variety of models which can be generated from simple mechanics, each of which may be as similar as one chooses to individual empirical cases. This offers the possibility of exact explanation and prediction for a great diversity of empirical events. But empirical generalization cannot do this, because exact prediction requires the precise replication of a known case as the basis for the general statement of empirical knowledge. Empiricist knowledge, when exact, is therefore very limited in scope.

The problem with modern systematic empiricism is not so much that it is empiricism (rather than science), but that it attempts to do what it cannot do—generate empirical knowledge of broad scope. But to cover a broad scope knowledge must subsume diverse and dissimilar empirical cases; however, the more dissimilar the cases subsumed by generalization, the more vague it becomes and the less valuable it is for predictive purposes.

Science and empiricism differ also in the manner in which each forms a system of knowledge. Empiricism is systematic in that it consistently maintains observation as the sole basis of thought connection and in that it may systematically develop its techniques for generalization; but its individual statements cannot be rationally connected, and thus they form *independent* bits of knowledge. We may observe that cold causes radiators to break, balls cause windows to break, heat causes plates to break, collisions cause automobiles to break, and social stress causes personalities to break; but, although each of these causal statements is concerned with breakage, they are otherwise unrelated. Each forms an independent explanation.

Science is a system of knowledge because of its consistent use of a combination of empirical, rational, and abstractive connection in gathering and applying knowledge; but it is systematic also in the integration of its explanatory statements into a rationalized whole. This interconnection of parts is possible in science because of its rational component. A continuing rationalization of parts means that science is developmental and that the scope and consistency of its explanatory statements may be further extended. One law may explain diverse observational phenomena, and its integration with another law in a rational system extends the scope of application of both. Furthermore, rational development may lead to a new theoretical statement capable of more precise or more inclusive explanation through either a simpler statement, better isomorphism with empirical phenomena, or extended scope. Increased isomorphism of theoretical statement and phenomena or increased scope of application means increased scientific power. The empirical division of science into widely separated fields according to subject matter ignores its nature as a system of knowledge and also limits its rationalization.

In contrast, empiricism develops only in the quantity of facts gathered and in the improvement of techniques for gathering them. The knowledge gained, however, forms a vast, unconnected mass similar to the mass formed by a pile of apples—each apple still remains an independent apple. By its very definition, empiricism is unable to rationalize its findings.

In the confusion of science with empiricism in everyday discourse, we frequently find diverse concerns such as physical science, military science, agricultural science, and social science all referred to as "science"; but many of these terms (military and agricultural science, for example) refer simply to a set of techniques and a body of empiricist knowledge. In this context the body of knowledge of military techniques should be referred to as military empiricism. Clearly any body of knowledge characterized by generalization and lacking in rationalization and an abstractively defined universe of application does not fit the definition of science.

Because of the common use of empiricism in the gathering of knowledge upon which to base daily actions, it is possible to point to scientific roots in empiricism. Biology was at one time no more than fact gathering, and chemistry was limited to trial-and-error laboratory procedures. This "natural history stage" of scientific development (as Stephen Toulmin calls it) may consist of a "let's see what will happen if . . ." approach, eventually leading to an attempt to construct a rational explanation when that approach fails to result in a determinative explanation. A theory which is successful in laboratory applications may be applied outside the test setting because its rational conditions of nonlimited scope permit it to be extended to any object in a universe defined by that scope. New scientific research is then not intended to uncover new relations; new relations are derived through theoretical calculation. In fact, the outcome of scientific research is expected not because it is common knowledge but because it is a determinative consequence of the theory. Lack of success in the use of a theory does not mean that the theory was false or wrong, but may instead indicate a limit to its scope (as in the case of Newtonian theory, which is used successfully to build bridges but cannot be used to explain the bending of light rays), or mean that an abstractive error was made, an error of interpretation.

Empirical research may precede scientific development but it does not necessarily do so. Timing the fall of a variety of objects such as leaves, paper, cannon balls, rocks, boards, and automobiles running off cliffs has little (if any) utility for the development of a useful theory of falling bodies. One could run correlations between the weight of such objects and their time of fall for many lifetimes without ever accumulating the sort of knowledge conducive to theoretical thinking about falling bodies. Although modern empirical methods are highly refined and complex their nature is unchanged. When engineering has been associated with science it has been more effective, and technological developments (using the results of scientific knowledge for empiricist effects) have frequently led to a confusion of technology with science. This empiricist use of scientific knowledge has not only added to the power of modern empiricism (increased success in material action), but it has also added to the confusion of empiricism with science which is so misleading to scholars trying to develop science in new areas.

The theory of knowledge defines science in such a way that those fields described as scientific in everyday discourse do not necessarily fit the definition. It remains then to consider the nature of knowledge in sociology from this perspective. Clearly the theoretical conception of science corresponds to some areas of knowledge which have developed laws and theories, but are the social sciences really scientific, or are they empiricist?

Because this analysis of science is a logical construction, it presents a scientific point of view toward science; but to understand much of this book it is necessary to understand the empiricist attitude toward science. From this point of view, science is a particular form of empiricism in which observations are systematically made and recorded. Thus, the empiricist's point of view toward science may be called "systematic empiricism." "Concepts" must be observable categories, and "abstraction" must be equivalent to generalization. Figure 5 compares the empiricist's notion of the structure of science with the structure of science as a knowledge system.

In Figure 5 you can see the empiricist's "leader of abstraction." The connections A_1 to B_1, and so forth, represent particular observed relations between A and B while A_n——B_n represents the empirical generalization which summarizes them. Regardless of how general the A_n——B_n relation, however, it is not abstract in the sense that the a——b relation is abstract. It is not abstractively

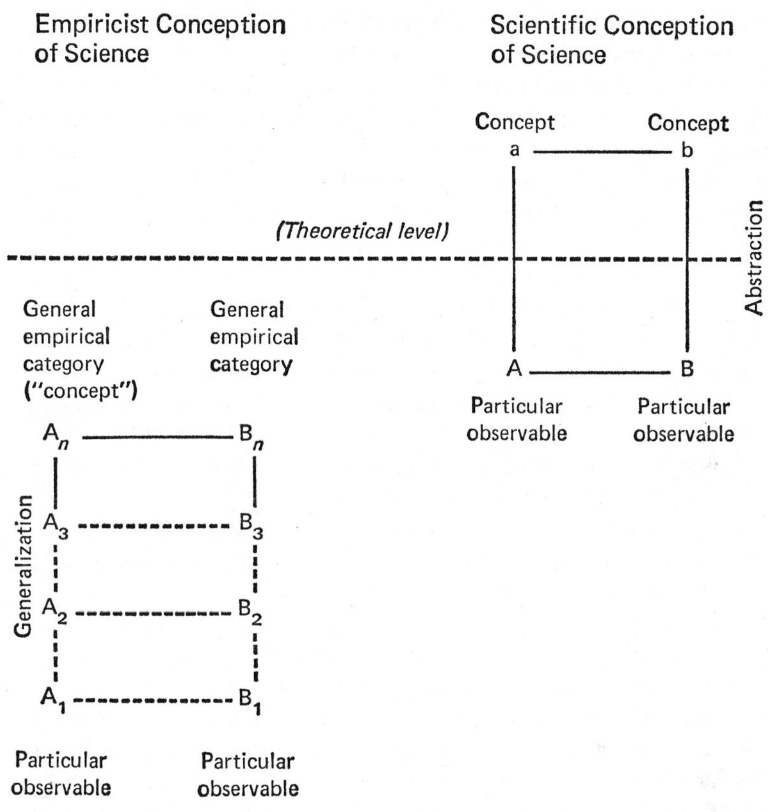

FIGURE 5. Comparison of the structure of science from empiricist and scientific points of view

related to particular observations but is a summary of them, and new observed relations are not explained, but subsumed, by it. Although there is no similarity between these generalizations and scientific laws, in either the terms or the manner in which they are connected, the empiricist mistakes the process of generalization for abstraction, and mistakes general statements for laws. Social empiricists may eventually obtain knowledge corresponding to their conception of science, but they will never obtain either the abstractive or rational components of science. It is therefore of importance whether the methods used in sociology and other social sciences will lead to science or merely to systematic empiricism.

the origins of systematic empiricism

3 One of the consequences of graduate training in sociology is a remarkable ignorance of the history of sociology and (perhaps less remarkable) of the history of the development of the sciences. The belief is prevalent that the most systematic methods of sociology are a direct outgrowth of the scientific tradition, which began with the works of Galileo and Kepler. Although modern science may indeed be traced to those sources, the methods actually used in sociology have a much shorter history. At the middle of the last century the meaning of science was interpreted and misunderstood by the British empiricist John Stuart Mill, who believed that science was identical to empiricism and attempted to provide a systematic framework by means of which science could be generated from empiricist techniques. Although he failed to do this, he did produce various systematized empirical procedures and may be regarded as the "Father of Systematic Empiricism." Historically, systematic empiricism has led not to science but to more systematic empiricism and, as such, proceeds from fact gathering to empirical generalization rather than to abstraction and rationalization. Mill's methods did not, in fact, work, for they did not even

lead to empirical knowledge. But, since then, the British Statistical School has contributed techniques which are believed to have solved the main problems inherent in Mill's methods. The development of this school, insofar as it affects the methods of sociology, can be understood as an attempt to correct the failings inherent in Mill's approach.

The Empirical Methods of John Stuart Mill

The history of systematic empiricism begins with John Stuart Mill and is thus little more than one hundred years old. Unlike Hume, whose concern was with the general problem of the basis of human knowledge, Mill was concerned specifically with the method of science. He developed a method of systematic empiricism in which his main concern was with *propositions*. Following Kant's distinction between analytic and synthetic propositions, Mill accepted only synthetic statements as "real propositions" because they are based on facts. Synthetic propositions are, in fact, empirical statements based on the association of sense impressions, while analytic propositions concerned with the association of ideas are rational statements.

Mill recognized the rational connection of idea with idea in analytic statements and the empirical connection of observation with observation in synthetic statements, but he did not recognize the possibility of abstractive connection of observation with idea. Consequently, for Mill, rational and empirical thought remain completely separated; and, because he realized that science has an empirical component, he discarded rational thought as a component of science. In order to include mathematics as a component of science, Mill was forced to argue that it is arrived at through generalization from particular observations. Even then, Mill's empirical method had little or no use for mathematics. Indeed, mathematics (as a rational system) cannot be incorporated in a method which systematically uses only empirical connection.

Mill begins with a discussion of *terms*. All terms that are the objects of synthetic propositions he calls concepts. His definition of a concept is obviously very different from that used here, for

Mill's "concepts" refer to classes of objects rather than to theoretically defined terms. Mill's terms are formed by a comparison of a set of objects in which all objects to be classified by a term demonstrate a *likeness* in some characteristic or property. His concepts are no more than empirical categories referring to observationally similar objects. Cow, bull, Negro male, Buick Electra, Catholic, and phonograph record are all concepts from Mill's point of view because they all are terms which stand for a set of objects having similar characteristics.

Mill unfortunately also referred to scientific concepts such as *mass, temperature,* and *energy* as concepts in *his* sense of the term. Although this results in treating the terms *cow, mass, Negro male, energy, Catholic,* and *temperature* as conceptually identical it is a necessary result of Mill's empiricist viewpoint.

Mill called the method of relating these "empirical concepts" in a real proposition "induction." "Induction, then, is that operation of the mind by which we infer that what we know to be true in a particular case or cases, will be true in all cases which resemble the former in certain assignable respects."[1] In other words, induction consists of making an inference that the knowledge we have of some empirical cases will be true at all times for all similar cases. The inductive procedure is therefore "Generalization from Experience."[2] Hume justified this procedure on a pragmatic basis: because the future is not unlike the past, repetition of past events is a satisfactory basis for knowledge and action. But Mill justified his empirical method by the assumption of uniformity in nature. He arrived at this assumption by an inductive process in which the accumulation of inductions of individual uniformities in nature leads to the all-encompassing induction that nature is uniform. To justify individual inductions, Mill argued from an induction based on them. He justified induction by induction. Mill's followers have sometimes recognized the futility of this circular argument, however, and turned back to Hume's pragmatism for support for their procedures. Nevertheless, many sociologists have

[1] John Stuart Mill, *A System of Logic* (London: Longmans, Green and Co., 1967), p. 188.

[2] *Ibid.*, p. 200.

acted on the assumption that the scientific method seeks out uniformities in nature.

Science, on the other hand, does not consist of statements about natural regularities. The regularities that we perceive are never invariant enough to justify the absolute connection of the equals sign often used in theoretical statements. On the contrary, scientific laws are not reflections of observed regularities. An assumption of regularity in nature is not necessary in science. Mill, however, was concerned with the construction of systematic empirical method to arrive at absolute empirical generalizations.

Mill assumed that the universe consists of absolute causal regularities. But he believed that many small empirical regularities overlap each other in common observation and frequently give the appearance of irregularity. But, if we sorted out all the confounding causal regularities for any particular empirical phenomenon which we wished to explain, we should be able to isolate the real regular cause. Mill's method is a method for *systematically sorting* one uniformity from others by using empirical controls. In this way "latent" regularities may be made "manifest" by sorting individual regularities from the general uniformity of the universe. Methods of elaboration, latent structure analysis, and factor analysis are successors to Mill's method, for they consist of sorting processes intended to isolate underlying or latent regularities by sorting among apparent irregularities.

According to Mill, the natural uniformities that would be discovered by his methods are "laws." These laws are of two types, those having the characteristic of simultaneous relationship and those characterized by successive relationship. Causation is concerned with successive relationship and is governed by the "Law of Causation" (a notion borrowed from Aristotle), which means that any fact with a beginning has a cause. A cause is the sum of the conditions from which an event necessarily follows. These causes are then to be discovered by the use of Mill's experimental method or "canons of proof." These canons describe the techniques to be used to sort causal relations from the assumed universe of general regularities. The canons have special significance in sociology where they still form the basis for the isolation of "findings" whether or not these findings are described as causal. The first canon, "the method of agreement," states that, in two experimental situations, if a number of conditions (*A, B, C,* and so on) are followed by an event (*a*) in the first situation, and if a number of conditions different in all cases but one (*A, G, H,* and so on) are followed by the same event (*a*) in the other situation, then only the condition shared by both experimental situations can be part of an invariant causal sequence. Mill then concluded that that shared condition (*A*) is causally connected with the event (*a*). The condition appearing first (*A*) is the cause, and the event (*a*) is the effect, both having been sorted from the multitude of cause–effect relations in the universe.

One might, for example, set up a typical sociological experiment in group norms in which the intent is to discover whether an individual's response to stimuli is affected by the response of others. In this case, we have antecedent conditions: *A,* the stated perceptions of other group members (who have previously been instructed to agree in their judgments about the relative length of a set of lines); *B,* the sex of the group members (all male in this case); and *C,* the actual set of lines of varying lengths to be judged by the observers as longer or shorter. In the first test *A, B,* and *C* are followed by *a,* the judgment by the individual that a particular line is shortest in conformity with the agreement of the group but contrary to the actual measured length of the line. In the second test condition *D* is substituted for *B* (the sex of the stooge group is now female) and the line lengths are altered to condition *E.* Here too the conditions are followed by *a.* Therefore, only *A* has been related to *a* in both cases, and *B, C, D,* and *E* can not form a part of an invariant causal sequence. Further tests may eliminate more variables (*F, G, H, I, J, K, L, M,* and any others the imaginative experimenter can think of), and one may conclude that *A* was the cause of (or a necessary condition for) *a.* (Obviously a too fertile imagination might prevent this method from ever isolating the real cause.)

Mill's second canon—the method of difference—is designed to strengthen a causal relationship such that *A* becomes not only a necessary but also a sufficient condition for effect *a.* In this type of experiment of *A, B,* and *C* are antecedent conditions which were followed by *a* in the first experiment, and if *B, C,* and *F* were not followed by *a* in a second experiment, then *A* is the cause of *a* and a sufficient condition for it. To continue our sociological experiment, we may substitute the condition *F* (for *A*) in which the group members do not agree on the length of the shortest line. Whereas *A*, *B*, and *C* were followed by *a*, we now find that *B*, *C*, and *F* are not. Mill would then conclude that *A* is a sufficient cause of effect *a*, and the sociologist would conclude that he has discovered a "causal finding." The sociologist, however, does not proceed under the assumption that the relations he finds are invariant in spite of his use of Mill's methods. In practice, perfect relationships are not found.

Mill's methods suffer from several practical difficulties. Even if one could assume perfect regularities in the universe, they might never be isolated because measurement error alone would result in less than perfect relationships once the variables were apprehended and recorded. On the other hand, if the universe consists of webs of interconnected causes, it may be impossible to control for all possible conditions that might affect the strength of the perceived relationship. Sociological research does not lead to invariant relational statements but to tendency statements. The experiment previously discussed could be represented as in Table 1.

TABLE 1. Effect on individual judgment (*a* or *f*) of agreement (*A*) or disagreement (*F*) of other group members

	a	*f*
A	20	5
F	5	20

The table represents the results of fifty cases, and it reveals that *A* is usually followed by *a* and that when *A* is absent *a* usually is also. Mill's method of agreement is used as the basis of interpretation even though the data are not invariantly related. In fact, the responses might have been affected by such factors as poor eyesight, indigestion, disagreeable personalities, or antagonism toward the study, and we might never achieve a perfect relationship because we cannot ever be sure we have controlled for all possible causes. We are left with the problem of determining a point at which we will believe that we have found a real causal relationship, and at that point we arbitrarily attribute any deviations from the real cause to the chance action of other causes (although Mill did not include the hypothesis of chance causes in his method).

Mill's third canon—the joint method of agreement and difference—is often used in sociological elaboration analysis. For example, the variables in Table 2 may be as follows:

a = completion of college
b = noncompletion of college
A = income of student's parents more than $10,000
B = income of parents less than $10,000
C = white
D = nonwhite

TABLE 2. Mill's joint method illustrating percentage of several variables related to college completion

		a	*b*
A	*C*	24	5
	D	26	4
B	*C*	4	16
	D	5	14

In this case *a* occurs with almost equal frequency under conditions *AC* and *AD*, and we would conclude through the method of agreement that *A* (rather than *C* or *D*) is a necessary condition for *a*. Using the method of difference we note that noncompletion (*b*) is far more common under condition *B* and completion less common, while again *C* and *D* appear to have little effect. This indicates that *A* is sufficient for *a*. We conclude that of the variables studied only *A* (parental income) is related to *a* (college completion). To achieve a more perfect relationship, however, we need to add more controls and to gather more facts to sort.

Mill's fourth canon—the method of residues—is another sorting procedure. In this method, we take an observed empirical phenomenon and a number of observed antecedent conditions, eliminate those antecedent conditions we know have certain effects on the phenomenon because of previous inductions, and consequently conclude that the remaining antecedent conditions are the causes of the "residue" effect (what is left over after the other effects have been sorted out). This procedure assumes that we have been able to make previous successful inductions, that our observation has included only causes and effects which are in fact universally connected, and that for any observed effect (or cause) its cause (or effect) has also been observed. In other words, we must have perfect powers of observation.

Mill illustrated this example with an explanation of the vibration in the oscillation of a pendulum. He began with the phenomena to be explained (the vibrating oscillating pendulum) and pointed out that we know that mountains disturb the smooth oscillation of pendulums. Consequently we remove the mountain as a cause and observe that our pendulum continues to vibrate, but more perfectly than before. Mill then suggested that ideally we should be able to remove the earth to determine what effect this might have. After enough causal elements have been sorted out, we will know what causes pendulums to vibrate without disturbance. Using this method in sociology we may, for example, explain the cause of voting conservatively if all causes of liberal voting are removed in the empirical cases we study. We may begin with a survey in which a population is classified according to the criteria rural or urban, rich or poor, and educated or uneducated. We find that urban people tend to be more liberal than rural ones, so we remove the urbanites and are left with the rural residue; then we find that the rich tend to be more liberal than the poor, so we eliminate wealth as a causal element; lastly we eliminate the educated because we find they tend to be more liberal than the uneducated. We are left with the antecedent conditions, rural, poor, and uneducated, as causes of conservative voting.

The problem with using the method of residues in sociology is that *we do not know any causal relations previous to the application of our survey.* We may find in our survey that being urban is associated with being liberal, but we do not know whether this is a causal relationship or, on the other hand, whether the voting preference is not the cause instead of the effect.

Mill's fifth canon—the method of concomitant variation—states that when two phenomena consistently vary at the same time, they are causally related. One phenomenon may be the cause and the other the effect, or they both may be related through some other variable or variables. For an observation of constant association of *A* and *a* this may not be a simple straightforward causal relationship, but both may be related to another antecedent condition *B* (which is the real cause), or an unobserved condition *C* (an intervening variable) may stand between *A* and *a*. (Or, in other words, we may never know the *real* cause!)

Mill considered the proposition that the reduction of velocity of objects is caused by friction in terms of the method of concomitant variation. He used the empirical case of a pendulum constructed so that its number of oscillations could be counted while varying the air pressure. The result of the experiment was that the number of oscillations increased as a vacuum was approached. Mill concluded that this experiment would result in Newton's first law of motion; air pressure was an intervening variable between limited motion and continuous motion. But the first law states that an object in motion will continue in uniform motion in a straight line unless an outside force acts on it. Mill's empiricist experiment could not lead to this scientific principle (which is not a law in the strict sense but a nonverifiable, a priori assumption); it could lead only to the conclusion that pendulums (which incidentally do not move in a straight line) oscillate a greater number of times in low air pressure. Because Mill did not observe forceless conditions, he could make no generalization about them. If we were to make general statements about pendulums and air pressure we would have to test several pendulums instead of just one. Such procedures could never lead to the formulation of laws. To arrive empirically at a general statement about all bodies, we would have to test all possible observable bodies, in a perfect vacuum, proceeding in a straight line; furthermore, we would have to experiment with them several times. In this case, we would indeed have to move the earth and, even more difficult, change its motion to a straight line and create a perfect vacuum around it.

Mill's methods are procedures for discovering natural causal laws by means of careful observation of nature. The result should be an absolute causal statement which is based on observed past regularities and assumes that the future will have the same regularities. A causal "law" states that some cause, an observed phenomenon *A*, always precedes some effect, an observed phenomenon *B*. Although sociologists make use of Mill's methods of proof, they do not believe that the observed regularities they find are absolute. Furthermore, modern statistical findings are usually considered sound only for the particular populations in which they are found.

In sociology we do not assume that if more rich students than poor ones graduated from college in the population we studied, this finding will be true for all populations. Such restriction on the application of empirical findings is the result of a more sophisticated empiricism, which recognizes that absolute true general statements cannot be made on the basis of limited past observation. To make absolute empirical generalization we would need the omniscient perception of God to make all observations of the phenomena for past, present, and future. Mill, however, did not possess such perfect perception, and his evidence that the universe is regular was based on the observation of such regularities as "all fires are hot" and "heavy bodies fall." *But these statements are not based on observed regularities at all, but rather on definition.* We would not call a body heavy if it did not fall, and we define fire by its heat. These are regularities only in the habitual use of such terms as *fire* and *hot.* Such statements are not synthetic but analytic. Thus they are not "real propositions" at all and cannot be confirmed or falsified by experience. Mill also used previously established scientific laws as examples of the regularity of the universe, but these laws were made by man rather than discovered by man and made by God. Indeed, only God (or an equivalent being or idea) would have the perception to discover such laws empirically. It is not surprising that sociologists using Mill's methods have discovered no laws.

Empiricism in sociology has, in fact, gathered data without uncovering any scientific laws; therefore, it has provided ample evidence of the futility of searching for laws through observation. On the basis of experience alone, Mill's claim of a regular universe seems implausible, but the empiricist always hopes that additional refinement of techniques of observation will eventually uncover such regularities.

Kingsley Davis and Wilbert Moore used an inference in the spirit of Mill in their claim that "all societies have stratification." The basis of this claim was the observation that all cases of societies with which they were acquainted had stratification structures; therefore, their statement should have been "all societies we know of have been stratified." Even if it were found that all societies with written histories were stratified, there is no assurance that societies without records had stratification structures. If, as Karl Marx claimed, history is written by educated upper classes, unstratified societies having no upper classes would not have left histories. Even if all past societies were stratified, our only statement could be "All past societies were stratified." We have no grounds for projection to the future. There are no empirical or logical grounds for assuming that the future will be like the past in this respect. In fact, the rational structure of theory in science does not imply that the future will be like the past (for that is an empirical question), but the necessary relations of terms in the theory mean that if in the future we will have measures for some terms we will be able to calculate values for the others. The results of empiricism, however, are stuck in the past, are concerned with the past, and have no necessary implications for the immediate present or future.

Statistical findings in sociology implicitly recognize the empirical limitations of empirical relationships. They are limited to particular times and places and are reports of research done which are related by likelihoods, do not claim nonlimited scope, and cannot be used for prediction. This represents an awareness of the limits of empiricism, but in practice it leads to an attempt to establish a predictive science without any basis for prediction.

Empirical generalization has three components: association, relation, and induction. Association involves the summary statement of individual facts and their connectives. Relation is the process of determining the extent and manner of connection of these facts. Induction is the process of extending the summary statement beyond the facts. Any empiricist method will provide methods of association, rules for relations, and techniques of induction as well as justification for each. Mill's method of association consisted of assigning labels to objects or events and to their connected consequences according to their observable *similarities.* Relation was either absolute or nothing, and induction was through stipulation that what was true for some cases will be true for all *similar* cases.

The British Statistical Influence

The British statisticians adopted from Mill an emphasis on the criterion of similarity but rejected the notion of absolute regularity in favor of probability or likelihood. Systematic empiricism (often confused with science) is concerned with generalization through Karl Pearson's methods of relation, R. A. Fisher's methods of association, and induction to a denumerable set (population) from a smaller randomly selected set (sample).[3]

Like Mill, Pearson confused science with empiricism, but Pearson's conception was more revolutionary. He challenged and rejected the view of science up to his time and substituted for it his own version of systematic empiricism, which he believed to be science. Mill tried to systematize empiricism into science and produced confusion, but Pearson's unadulterated empiricism produced a type of knowledge unlike science in any respect. In this sense Pearson's work represents the first clear separation of systematic empiricism from the older scientific tradition; however, like Mill, Pearson himself believed that science and empiricism were identical, and he did not intend to separate them but instead to provide a solid foundation for future scientific work.

According to Pearson, scientific laws are résumés—"*brief expression*[*s*] of the relationships and sequences." [4] Laws are generalizations,[5] and progress in science is identified with the discovery

[3] We could also mention Francis Galton, who extended empiricism from Mill's rigid position by combining it with an idea of probability, which was refined for empirical use by his student and colleague, Karl Pearson.

[4] Karl Pearson, *The Grammar of Science* (New York: Meridian Books, Inc., 1957), p. 82.

[5] *Ibid.,* p. 86.

of broader and broader generalizations. Although according to Mill laws were regularities in nature about which we make statements, to Pearson laws were the statements themselves, although they are concerned with relations and sequences. Pearson clearly realized that laws are products of human thought and contended that it is senseless to speak of the working of a law of nature, as laws are constructed by men. But Pearson failed to separate generalization from the abstraction of a scientific law. Nevertheless, because generalizations and laws are both human products, he was right, in spite of his confusion, that laws are not to be found in nature. But he was right for the wrong reasons.

The role of mathematics in science is difficult to explain from an empiricist view of science. Generalizations are synthetic, but mathematical statements are analytic. Thus, if the empiricist were to be consistent, he would have to argue that mathematics has no role at all in science; it makes no sense to state that a synthetic statement can be put in mathematical terms. Mill did not use mathematics in his method because the results of his method cannot be stated in terms of mathematical equalities. On the other hand, Pearson claimed that the use of an equals sign in scientific laws was for the purpose of connecting two numerically equivalent quantities. He asserted, however, that, because actual experience never shows an exact equivalence in any empirical relationship, mathematically stated laws misrepresent reality by claiming a higher level of relationship than can be justified by experience.[6] From his belief that laws are descriptive one may infer that laws stated in terms of mathematical equivalence are not accurate because they describe not actual experience but idealized cases. Pearson believed that mathematical laws are improperly conceived as invariant.

Pearson argued that because there is no necessity in experience, there should be no necessity in scientific laws, such as that implied by the use of an equals sign. To illustrate the lack of necessity in nature, he pointed out that he could himself follow an elliptical path around an object according to the law of gravity but would still be free at any time to change his mind and follow a path of another shape! [7] This example instead illustrates his complete lack

[6] *Ibid.*, pp. 97, 99.
[7] *Ibid.*, p. 135.

of understanding of the role of laws in science, particularly the law of gravity. The law does not state either that all elliptical paths are included in its scope or that following such a path is a matter of choice. Choosing another path does not negate the law of gravity, but if Pearson had remained suspended in the air after jumping (by an act of will?) we might indeed question its utility.

Pearson's problem is symptomatic of the empiricist approach to science in that empirical synthetic statements are not the same as rational analytic statements; and, if science is empiricist knowledge, analytic statements must be thrown out because we would otherwise contradict the assumption that statements may be either analytic or synthetic, but not both. This problem does not exist in a conception of science as containing not only an empirical component but a rational component tied to it by an abstractive component. A scientific law is accordingly stated mathematically in rational form and applied to observationals through abstractive connections. Observationals are related through abstraction to concepts, through rational calculation (in terms of mathematical relations) to other concepts, and in turn to other observationals. Empiricists, however, mistake abstraction for generalization and view a general empirical relation as abstract. From this narrow point of view there is no way to get from observationals to mathematically stated laws. Mathematics can have no utility in the empiricist view of science (for relating terms), and for this reason statistics are used instead.

Pearson rejected mathematical connectives, distrusted the use of concepts, and argued that experience should form the sole basis of a scientific method. Empirical relations are never invariant, and mathematical laws do not reflect experience. According to Pearson, science does not explain anything but is merely a "shorthand description" used simply to facilitate economical thought.[8] Thus, science merely helps us think if we are either too lazy or too limited in our mental capacity to handle the more accurate details of experience. (Although this is not true for science it is, in fact, true for empiricism!)

If laws are conceived of as empirical generalizations, then some

[8] *Ibid.*, p. xi.

method of induction must be presented so that our past experiences may be used to anticipate future events. "That the future will be like our experience of the past is the sole condition under which we can predict what is about to happen and so guide our conduct." [9] Science is therefore a description of the past coupled with a faith that the future will be the same. Pearson supplements this faith with a generalization in the style of Mill: "The overwhelming probability drawn from past experience in favor of all sequences repeating themselves at once embraces the new sequence." [10] Pearson does not assume that the universe is absolutely regular, but that its irrgularity is regular; therefore, sequences are probable rather than absolute, but the probability is stable.

Pearson wished to put an end to the domination of experience by concepts and to replace it with a domination of experience over "concepts." [11] The relationships of science should, therefore, be relations of *things,* not of concepts, and the categories should simply be terms that stand for things. Things are grouped into categories because they are similar, and the basis of category formation is not identity of objects but "likeness." [12] Scientific terms, according to Pearson, are defined ostensively by the observations included in them. This view is at least an improvement over that of other empiricists in that it takes into account the lack of identity of objects in nature.

If two or more empirical objects can never be identical, then two different causal sequences can never be identical, and therefore, in Pearson's view, scientific relationships cannot be based on identity or equivalence: "You cannot get exactly the like causes." [13] Scientific laws or generalizations consequently must be stated as probabilities, and relations of things can be represented by a number through correlation or contingency: "No phenomena are causal; all phenomena are contingent, and the problem before us is to measure the degree of this contingency, which we have seen lies

[9] *Ibid.,* p. 136.

[10] *Ibid.,* p. 141.

[11] *Ibid.,* p. 165.

[12] *Ibid.,* p. 170.

[13] *Ibid.,* p. 154.

between the zero of independence and the unity of causation."[14] As a result, "the fundamental problem of science is to discover how the variation in one class is correlated with or contingent on the variation in a second class."[15]

With no false modesty, Pearson claimed that his conception of the universe, replacing causation by contingency and correlation, was "epoch-making."[16] He urged physicists to return from the conceptual world to reality by adopting his ideas. He took a stand in direct opposition to Mill's idea of causation. Although it may indeed by true that empirical events are never identical and empirical relations are never equivalent, Pearson has asked us to adhere to a position no less fantastic than the empiricist assumption that nature is uniform, that from observation of unlike objects and their relationship to other unlike objects in terms of unstable correlations and contingencies we can predict the future and regulate our behavior and environment.

Pearson's methods are similar to Mill's in that observation is the central element. Terms are both defined and related by observation, although causation has been replaced by correlation and contingency. Empirical categories are related to other empirical categories at particular levels of correlation and contingency which are determined by the results of observations. Pearson did not tell us the scope of application of his contingent empirical generalizations, but we can conclude that, insofar as he based his ideas on Hume's, he intended them to have unlimited scope with the qualification that if the future were found to be unlike the past, new research would be needed.

Although he rejected the idea of scientific explanation, Pearson believed that his science based on uncertainty could predict the future. From Pearson's point of view all things must be related at least a little (somewhere between a probability of zero and one) because the rejection of absolute relationships in nature includes not only absolute dependence of cause and effect but also absolute independence. From Mill's point of view, a relationship exists either absolutely or not at all (one disconfirming case being suffi-

[14] *Ibid.*, p. 174.

[15] *Ibid.*, p. 165.

[16] *Ibid.*

cient to falsify it), but when relationships are thought to range between zero and one then the researcher is left with the problem of deciding which are "real" and which may be discounted as "chance" (unless he accepts them all as real).

If the universe is conceived as a system of interrelated probable relationships, knowledge could never be accurate until everything in the universe is correlated and measured; yet we cannot measure the future, which is only probably like the past. Pearson's empiricism, therefore, can never result in true knowledge despite his claim that its purpose is to take us from the inaccurate knowledge of concepts to the true knowledge of observation.

The determination of *association* of empirical observationals should be made before the determination of the extent of relationship. Pearson's method is incomplete in that he ignored the problem of determining association entirely and as a consequence did not provide a method that could result in generalization. Fisher provided a statistical solution to the problem of association which could be used with Pearson's method of relation and already developed methods of induction to arrive at the finished product of modern statistical empiricism, a "probabilistic" empirical generalization.

Fisher approached the problem of determining association through a method of statistical testing developed from the theory of errors based on the work on mathematical probability of the seventeenth and eighteenth centuries. The equation for the normal curve was developed by DeMoivre as a result of his concern with the binomial theorem. This was consequently used in astronomy in an attempt to explain variations in data, and by 1832 processes were developed by Encke for the computation of the standard error of the mean and standard deviation.[17] Fisher subsequently adapted the theory of errors to statistical testing.

Although Fisher's justification of statistical testing was based on the theory of errors, its actual use was not dependent upon an a priori probability theory. Nevertheless, Fisher himself explained his method with an example in which a priori calculation is possible.

[17] See Helen M. Walker, *Studies in the History of Statistical Method* (Baltimore: Waverly Press, 1929), p. 25.

In his attempt to attain "natural knowledge" by experience (or synthetic knowledge), Fisher argued that statistical procedure and experimental design are two aspects of the same whole.[18] (This might have been a surprise to Galileo.) Fisher described his method of empirical association as a process of inference "from observations to hypotheses; as a statistician would say from a sample to the population." [19] Fisher would not accept the argument that we cannot infer from the particular to the general: "We may at once admit that any inference from the particular to the general must be attended with some degree of uncertainty, but this is not the same as to admit that such an inference cannot be absolutely rigorous." [20] The rigor involved in inferences of this sort is a result of the "rigorous" calculation of the degree of uncertainty. Rigorous uncertainty is the desired result of Fisher's process of associational inference.

Fisher believed that new knowledge could be gained only through generalization using an experiment which consists of no more than "experience carefully planned in advance." [21] As a true empiricist, he dogmatically rejected "dogmatic data" and argued for the liberation of the human intellect by direct observation, or what he referred to as "experimental science." [22] Fisher did not concern himself with the development of scientific laws but directed his efforts to the examination of "the principles which are common to all experimentation." [23] These principles, he claimed, were most carefully worked out in agriculture. Here he neatly disposed of centuries of scientific work in favor of the techniques of his own field, agriculture. If the physicists had only followed the methods of agriculture, they might now possess some real knowledge.

He illustrated the value of his method and the principles com-

[18] See R. A. Fisher, *The Design of Experiments* (London: Oliver and Boyd, 1935), p. 3.

[19] *Ibid.*, p. 4.

[20] *Ibid.*

[21] *Ibid.*, p. 9.

[22] *Ibid.*, p. 10.

[23] *Ibid.*, p. 11.

mon to all experimentation with an examination of the taste-discriminating powers of a lady tasting tea:

> A lady declares that by tasting a cup of tea made with milk she can discriminate whether the milk or the tea infusion was first added to the cup. We will consider the problem of designing an experiment by means of which this assertion can be tested. . . . Our experiment consists in mixing eight cups of tea, four in one way and four in the other, and presenting them to the subject for judgment in a random order. . . . Her task is to divide the eight cups into two sets of four, agreeing, if possible, with the treatments received.[24]

If there are eight cups and four choices to be made it is possible to calculate a priori that there are seventy ways of choosing four objects out of eight. Thus, if each alternative were equally likely, the probability of choosing the four right cups is one in seventy. The experiment itself has been made in order to either justify or reject the claim. The chance that her choice would be accurate was one in seventy. At this point the *null hypothesis* enters the experiment. The null hypothesis, in this case, states that the lady's judgments were *not* influenced by the order in which the tea and milk were put into the cup. The null hypothesis is justified because "every experiment may be said to exist only in order to give the facts a chance of disproving the null hypothesis."[25] According to Fisher, the null hypothesis provides "the basis of the 'problem of distribution.'"[26] The example of the lady's cups of tea unfortunately cannot be easily used to illustrate the problem of distribution, so another of Fisher's examples will be used at this point.

Darwin had claimed that cross-fertilized plants were superior to self-fertilized ones but was unable to prove it. Following Galton, Fisher proposed an experiment to measure superiority by the height of plants. Two sets of plants, one self-pollinated and the other cross-pollinated, were measured for height. Fisher then asked

[24] *Ibid.*, pp. 13–14.

[25] *Ibid.*, p. 19. This statement is itself a "universal" empirical generalization, which is false if it is not definitional and, if definitional, is not a generalization.

[26] *Ibid.*

whether the heights could be considered the same in order to test the null hypothesis that they were in effect the same population. If their variations in height were randomly distributed (and thus empirically like errors of measurement of an object), then it could be concluded that the populations were essentially the same in height. The purpose of the test was to determine how unlikely it was that the height differences were randomly distributed, the mean of the cross-pollinated group being higher, as Darwin had anticipated. The test was a test for randomness, and the result was "that it was unlikely that the data were random." Here, as in modern research, the conclusion is reached that it is likely that the data are nonrandom.

The test of randomness is a test of data, not of association. The test results not in a statement that the association between cross-pollination and self-pollination was not likely to be random, but in a statement that the difference between the height of the two populations was not likely to be random. It was not the association between cross-pollination and a taller yield which was directly tested and found, even though the cross-pollinated population was significantly different in height from the self-pollinated population after the experiment. As far as the test itself is concerned, any other association of empirical factors with height is just as likely. The experimenter concerned himself with only one of a possible infinity of elements that could be related to the nonrandom distribution of height of the plants. The null hypothesis is often *stated* in terms of the elements varied in the experiment; but those elements are not entailed in the actual test, which is concerned only with the likelihood of randomness of the data. We might as easily conclude that the height of plants is associated with almost any empirical fact, such as the average height of soldiers in the American and British armies. We could have just as legitimately stated a null hypothesis that the height of plants in the two populations was not related to the differential in height of American and British soldiers. Although the empirical association of soldiers and height of plants is rather farfetched, we could just as correctly infer that association as the one concerned with cross-pollination because in actuality we have tested only data randomness. From the test, we can infer nothing at all. Rejecting the null hypothesis in either case means simply that it is unlikely that the differences in height are random—it tells us nothing about what particular association is not random. Occasionally an experimenter will state his null hypothesis simply in terms of the randomness of the data; but, although this accurately reflects the results of the actual test, still no conclusion can be drawn about some positive or, in Fisher's terms, "opposed hypothesis." *Any inference made of an association between variables in such an experiment cannot result from the test of the null hypothesis itself but must come from elsewhere, principally from the intent of the experimenter in designing his experiment and consequently determining his controls.* The test of significance is no more than a legitimization for an association either already evident by inspection or already intended by the researcher.

On the other hand, the test of significance cannot be extended beyond affirmations of randomness or nonrandomness without making an elementary logical error. The researcher who believes that if the null hypothesis is true, the manipulation is effective, cannot conclude anything at all about the effectiveness of the manipulation if the null hypothesis is false. If A implies B, then one cannot conclude anything about B from the negation of A. Thus Fisher's null hypothesis design actually provides no basis for relating the rejection of the null hypothesis to the possibility of association.

Now let us return to the lady tasting tea (if she still has any tasting ability left). If the experiment is to be adequate, all of the cups should be identical except for the characteristic tested. Residues of soap in some cups and not in others might have undesired effects on her ability to discriminate. But assurance of such perfect control, as Pearson had explained earlier, is not possible because the things of our experience may be similar but never identical. Fisher pointed out that the cups may differ in texture and thickness and the tea in strength, but there are many other possible ways in which differences may enter into the experiment. In any experiment, in fact, it would be impossible to list all of the ways that possibly relevant conditions might vary and thus interfere with the results. Fisher claimed that this problem is common to all experimentation. Although our best efforts may result in the partial equalization of some conditions, others would remain uncontrolled. Partial equalization may not be satisfactory and may give spurious results.

Fisher attempted to solve this problem by randomizing the selection of objects to be used in the experiment. Thus, the lady's cups must be ordered at random, the infusion ordered randomly, and anything else which could possibly affect the outcome should be randomized—everything but the original manipulation (in this case infusion of milk first in half of the cups and tea first in the other half). Fisher also discussed more conventional types of controls and pointed out that the lady might object if some tea were Chinese and some Indian, or if some milk were raw and some boiled. Gross differences of that sort should be controlled if the test is to be sensitive to the experimental manipulation.[27] In fact, the problem still exists; we can never know if we have randomized and systematically controlled all relevant variables.

The tea-tasting experiment is different from most applications of significance tests in that the probability could be calculated a priori. Usually such prior calculation is not possible in experiments. To solve this problem, Fisher introduced the idea of fiducial probability in which the observed statistics, such as the mean and standard deviation, are used to estimate the unknown parameters and the distribution of the statistics to calculate the probability.[28]

The immediate aim of Fisher's method was practical. Most of his examples were drawn from his agricultural research and were concerned with questions such as "Which of two grains will yield more in this type of soil with this amount of sun and water?" Clearly his method had implications beyond that. If it is assumed that it is possible to test for a difference between means, then it is logically possible to test whether a correlation or contingency is likely due to chance. This provides the decision criteria needed to accept or reject a correlation and thus provides the empiricist with a legitimization for his claim of association. Empiricist researchers consequently had a basis on which to accept or reject relationships according to a neatly dichotomous criterion. This criterion for

[27] *Ibid.*, p. 28.

[28] See Chapter 7 of this book for a discussion of fiducial probability.

association has been considered of such great importance in sociology that, for all practical purposes, conventional research is no longer concerned with levels of relationship and is now interested only in whether associations are significant—that is, whether null hypotheses are unlikely to be random. Furthermore, as long as the Fisher method is limited to the experimental setting, spurious associations can be controlled by manipulation and randomization. It is the ease of control by randomization which makes the procedure practical.

Control through randomization is also relevant to Mill's objection to the use of "inductive methods" in social science. Mill argued that social science is impossible because too many controls are necessary. Control by randomization is nevertheless much simpler and can be used more extensively than Mill imagined.

Fisher set out to provide a rigorous foundation for association—for inferences from the particular facts to a summary statement about them. Such inferences are justified by the test of the null hypothesis, and indeed result in "rigorous uncertainty." Even if the association were logically entailed in the test (which it is not), its scope is limited to the facts upon which it is based. For Fisher's agricultural research this problem was easily solved because his experimental objects, such as strains of seeds, had been previously manipulated and selected into separate homogeneous strains. One strain of seed could be considered to be essentially identical to another because of their careful development following genetic laws. Fisher's induced associations were at least partly dependent on scientific laws and thus were actually not inductive as all but simply demonstrated an expected isomorphism. Fisher could argue for the sameness of his experimental objects because they were developed according to the dictates of genetic theory. In sociology, our empirical subjects are obviously not of that type. While Fisher had the perfect control provided by the use of laws, we can only randomize our selection of subjects and hope that it is relevant. Whereas Fisher's experiments merely confirmed Darwinian theory and Mendelian laws, sociology is left in the circumstance in which there are no such laws to confirm. Yet it is evident that Fisher did not understand the crucial role played by science as it determined the effectiveness of his method in agriculture. Instead he attributed the effectiveness wholly to the design, a mistake which has been routinely made ever since.

Fisher's method of association completes the method of systematic empiricism. His design is, in Mill's terms, a method of difference proceeding from the assignment of objects to two or more groups, through manipulation of at least one, to measurement and the test of the null hypothesis. At this point an inference of positive association is made if the null hypothesis is denied. The inference that there is a difference between the means of the measured groups is meant to imply that the difference is associated with the different manipulations. This method of association is the first step in systematic empiricism.

The next step—the determination of the strength of relationship of the associated objects—uses a relational technique such as correlation or contingency. The final step—the induction of the related association beyond the facts studied—is justified either by running the same experiment in new similar circumstances, or, as is more common in sociology, by inducing to a population from a tested sample of it. In that case, the similarity of the sample to the population is determined by its random selection. Although there is justification for this approach to induction, it clearly imposes limitations of scope.

If an experiment is run several times using controls established by a scientific law, as in Fisher's case, the association can be extended to a potentially unlimited number of cases. In fact, that is a characteristic of scientific laws. Fisher's main problem was that he realized neither that his associations were simply applications of laws, nor that their scope of further application was based on laws and not on inductive inference. The use of random samples for induction to populations is an implicit recognition within sociology and related fields that test–retest methods will not lead to universally true relationships. Induction from a sample to a population is indeed justified, but scientific laws having the characteristic of nonlimited scope can never be developed through this method.

The brilliance of the techniques and procedures of generalization developed by the statisticians is tarnished by their triviality. Fisher's example of the lady and her cups of tea is unfortunately typical of cases chosen for study. Who cares if a little old lady can tell tea from beer? What is the scientific value of such a problem? When applied to things not scientifically controlled, systematic empiricism is systematically concerned with trivia. We make associations between church attendance, age, political affiliation, economic value, crime rates, and so on and collect answers to numerous trivial questions on trivial questionnaires concerned with subjects such as whether we love our fathers or would "like to have Negroes living next door." What has this to do with science? This method is well suited to the study of trivia but not at all suited to the attainment of scientific knowledge, which does not deal with nose counts and prejudices. It is easy to see why sociology based on systematic empiricism is so trivial. Important issues are frequently ignored simply because they cannot be studied empirically, or if studied, they are reduced to trivia by the design of the study. The reduction of fascism to responses on an attitude scale (and thus to a personality characteristic) is but one case in point.

Systematic empiricism was eagerly adopted in newer "sciences" and passed off as science even though it did not have results at all similar to science. Pearson thought that laws and theories were gained by the inspired empiricism of great men (including himself). He was, like Galton, a confirmed elitist who promoted eugenics and believed the crude racist and classist tenets of social Darwinism. Actually, the stress on great men is a legitimization for the fact that laws and theories are not a direct result of the application of their method despite their claim that it is science. In fact, systematic empiricism needs no great men to do great thinking because it is a wholly mechanical process. Once one knows the procedures, no thought is required (or even desired).

Statistical empiricism, despite its trivial results, is at least superior to Mill's method, which was completely unworkable. Workability, however, entailed accepting rigorously uncertain association, less than absolute relations, and a narrow scope of induction. Modern enlightened empiricists at least realize that Mill's belief that association could be certain, relations absolute, and inductions universal, is wrong. Because of the uncertainty and limited scope of generalization resulting from systematic empiricism, its establishment as a method means that many people can be kept very busy without ever coming up with a single scientific law or theory.

the techniques of systematic empiricism

4 Sociology may be divided into three basic empirical approaches: (1) systematic empiricism developed from the statistical tradition; (2) participant observation, which is less systematic but has a certain unity of method resulting in a body of descriptive facts tied together by the locality in which the observation was made (sometimes called a "case study"); and (3) empirical theories, which are not rational systems of related concepts, as in science, but sweeping generalizations intended to be descriptive of empirical universals in society. These empirical "theories" reach a peak in "grand theories," which are so general (and thus vague) that their empirical relevance has long been open to criticism. They are frequently tied in with what is known as the "historical–comparative method," which is simply a process of searching for such patterns or "theories" in history. Ordinarily this method is used not so much to justify "theoretical" generalizations but to illustrate their meaning.

These three approaches determine what is considered legitimate knowledge in sociology today. Because of their procedures, these approaches are very different; consequently sociological empiricism is not narrow. Nevertheless, in spite of the intellectual battles and empirical claims made by their proponents, these approaches are identical in the sense that they are empiricist and thus narrow in their point of view toward what is legitimate knowledge in sociology. Empiricism, in fact, not only defines what is legitimate in sociology today but forms the basis for interpretation and criticism of the work of their predecessors (such as Marx, Weber, or Durkheim), often resulting in the opinion that their work is inadequate. Claims are made, for example, that Marxian theory cannot be used to explain modern capitalist economies because in Marx's day there were no television commercials and Marx thus said nothing about them and could not handle them with his theory. This is similar to claiming that Newtonian physics cannot be used for calculating the orbits of rockets because Newton had never seen a rocket.

The systematic empiricists, having the most sophisticated justification and the most mechanical procedures of the three approaches, have been dominant in sociology since the 1940s. But both theoretical empiricism and participant observation claim to be able to do things that systematic empiricism cannot do. Participant observation proponents claim, for example, that only their method can be used to arrive at a real understanding of what is really there because only in their method is the researcher intimately involved with his data. The result of the conflicting claims that one method of empiricism is better than others has been a balance of power between the authorities representing each group, either brightening or dimming the sociological scene—depending on one's point of view. These dialogues (between "hard" versus "soft" methodology, "theory" versus research, participant observation versus experimentation, experimentation versus survey research, and so on) unfortunately have only obscured the problems of sociological empiricism and have not resulted in a scientific method.

More and more sociologists have apparently come to believe that systematic empiricism is, in fact, the only way to true scientific knowledge in sociology. This system has continued the tradition of the British statistical school. Although American sociology has been empiricistic from its beginnings, it was not effectively systematized until recently. When the British statistical school solved the problems of systematic empirical generalization through the development of methods of association (through tests of significance), relation (through correlation and contingency), and induction (from random samples to populations), American empiricist sociology was ready.

Considering the preeminent position of systematic empiricism in sociology today, it is surprising that it is so young. It certainly was not used by W. I. Thomas and Florian Znaniecki in *The Polish Peasant.* It was not the method of the Chicago School of the twenties and thirties. The Lynds did not use it in *Middletown.* It was not the basis for the study of the Hawthorne plant. These, among the most famous works of early twentieth century sociology, were based on the empiricism of the participant observation–case study approach. They were concerned primarily with fact gathering and, when analytic, were not systematic. In fact, not until the study of *The American Soldier* did systematic empiricism form the basis of a major sociological study. Before then, surveys were descriptive only and experiments were seldom systematized. For this reason, *The American Soldier* represents a turning point in the development of American sociological methodology.

Early books on methodology further demonstrate that systematic empiricism was borrowed rather than internally developed. F. H. Giddings (writing in 1901 and 1924) presented a very unorganized picture of empiricist methodology which he based on an unsystematic aggregation of some ideas from Mill and Pearson.[1] He confused empirical generalization with laws, and concepts with empirical categories, and this confusion is retained in modern sociological empiricism. He thought science was based on the empirical observation of regularities. He presented no clear idea of how the process of generalization should proceed. His empiricism was so incomplete and unsystematic that he could not explain how research was to be done. Yet Giddings was considered important among the methodologists of his time. His writing is in sharp contrast with modern methods books, which outline, step by step, a mechanical process for carrying out research.

In 1931 Stuart Rice's *Methods of Social Science,* although it was

[1] See F. H. Giddings, *The Scientific Study of Human Society* (Chapel Hill, N.C.: The University of North Carolina Press, 1924) and *Inductive Sociology* (New York: The Macmillan Company, 1901).

consistently empiricistic, contained only nine of fifty-two sections which were even faintly related to systematic research, and none of those cites even one study using systematic empiricism. At that time most methods books were unsystematic, and most research involved the case-study approach. In a rare early example of a sociological survey—the West Coast race relations study organized by Robert Park in 1926—the analysis involved the use of correlation but no test of significance.

The attempt to trace modern systematic empiricism in sociology back to Charles Booth's survey work and Max Weber's German contemporaries is not justified. Early surveys were concerned only with fact gathering (and were recognized as such), and thus did not differ (except in scope) from state censuses whose history goes back at least to the Roman Empire. In contrast, sociological surveys carried out today are intended to be analytic in the sense that they are intended to establish relations among observables.

The history, or perhaps more accurately the *prehistory,* of systematic empiricism in sociology is concerned with the development of systematic methods of association, relation, and induction and was completed when Fisher provided a method of association by significance tests. Sociological empiricists then, as now, were concerned not with the logical problem of going from association to relation to induction to produce an empirical generalization but more with the practical problem of setting up a research design which could be followed absolutely, both making the process simpler and providing rigid standards in terms of which they can evaluate each other's work. Sociological empiricists have been more concerned with the techniques of procedure than with the logic of their methods; they consequently have little understanding of the differences between their methods and scientific ones.

The method of sociological experimentation used today differs only in a few elaborations from the method used by Fisher in his agricultural experiments, but it is hampered by the difficulty of manipulating certain social variables such as racial prejudice, organizational structure, religious beliefs, and legal systems. In fact, sociological empiricists have usually been able to manipulate only trivial things even when, as in the *American Soldier* studies, they were an integral part of a powerful bureaucracy. For this reason survey analysis was brought upon the scene. Here Mother Nature could do the "manipulating"; all the empiricist needed to do was to stand by and systematically record the results.

The survey method, especially the post-factum analysis of survey data, was intended to transform survey research into an analogy to the experiment using the already developed statistical techniques of association, relation, and induction. When these systematized methods of generalization were merged with the survey, the problem of experimental manipulation disappeared, and systematic empiricism through surveys became the predominant mode of sociological research.

Unlike Fisher, who was an agricultural technician not concerned with science, sociological empiricists have felt constrained to justify the adoption of statistical techniques because their method is expected to produce science. Their work had to be justified if they were to obtain support for it; therefore, they went backward to Mill's idea of causation. If empiricist procedures can be claimed to isolate causes, then financial support could be obtained from those who could cause things to happen (who, conveniently enough, were also those who had the money). Furthermore, the results were thought to be scientific because of the belief among empiricists that science results in causal statements.

Writers of sociological methods texts commonly state that statistical–empiricist methods result in causal relations.[2] In contrast, modern statistical works seldom mention causation.[3] The latter group, which usually determines the design of most systematic empiricist studies, is concerned with the establishment of associations rather than causal relations. Therein lies the dilemma. On the one hand, the empiricist sociologist wants to claim that his methods are capable of establishing certain absolute universal empirical generalizations of the form, *A* causes *B*; but, on the other hand, the actual design of his experiments and survey work fol-

[2] See, for example, W. J. Goode and Paul Hatt, *Methods in Social Research* (New York: McGraw-Hill Book Co., 1952), and M. W. Riley, *Sociological Research: A Case Approach* (New York: Harcourt Brace Jovanovich, 1963).

[3] See, for example, Allen L. Edwards, *Experimental Design in Psychological Research* (New York: Holt, Rinehart and Winston, Inc., 1950), and B. J. Winer, *Statistical Principles in Experimental Design* (New York: McGraw-Hill Book Co., 1962).

lows the procedures of statisticians and results in rigorous uncertainties, loosely related, and of limited scope. The result of mixing the ideas of Mill and those of the statisticians is confusion and contradiction, an unrationalized muddle which is obscured by the separation of logic and procedure.

Still, it would seem that our methodology texts are not found to be unpalatable even when we are served up the test of significance in the mistaken belief that it is a test of causation. Thus, a sociological finding may be called a causal relationship if its null hypothesis is unlikely to be due to chance. This confusion has been carried so far that the newly trained sociologist often assumes that the test of significance is a test of a positive (causal) hypothesis.[4] In the absence of an understanding of the difference between empiricism and science and of a real grasp of the implications of statistical empiricism, the faith in the value of causal–statistical empiricism can easily be propagated. Since few sociologists have ever been exposed to the meaning of science in their work, the belief comes easily. It legitimizes their work; and, although it is logically untenable, it is believed.

The Experiment

The purpose of the empiricist experiment in sociology and social psychology is to *find* an empirical generalization in the data. These generalizations are consequently referred to as *findings*. As Samuel Stouffer explained in a communication to his boss, General Osborn, "The only certain way to demonstrate that *A* has the effect *B* is by controlled experiment. Any other method contains a margin of error which may be considerable." [5] In the absence of control by the use of laws, the empiricist must control his experiment through empirical power alone. If the experimenter has the empirical power to create and manipulate the circumstances of his study and if he

[4] Blalock, on the other hand, attributes causality to the level of correlation. See Chapter 6 of this book for a discussion of Blalock's beliefs.

[5] Samuel A. Stouffer, "How These Volumes Came to Be Produced," in Stouffer et al., *The American Soldier: Adjustment During Army Life* (Princeton, N.J.: Princeton University Press, 1949), Vol. 1, p. 16.

has mastered the elementary techniques and procedures, the design of the empiricist experiment is simple. There is no need to formulate concepts, models, or formal theories, for there is no place for theoretic thought in the empiricist's experimenal design.

The experiment proceeds by the selection of an often conventional scaling technique, subjects to manipulate and respond, and means of control and manipulation. The academic empiricist may often choose his students, or the organizational or governmental bureaucrat the members of his bureaucracy, as subjects because of both his power position in relation to them and their easy availability. It is not always thought to be necessary to formulate a hypothesis (untested empirical generalization) before the experiment, and some empiricists even argue against it: "Intensive cultivation of an area of research by an alert observer will inevitably bring out interrelations among the phenomena comprising that area. The interrelations will take the form of similarities among the variables relevant to the different phenomena." [6] This is empiricism in its crudest form as distinguished from those who feel that it is necessary to test "theoretically relevant hypotheses" even though those hypotheses are no more than empiricist speculations composed of connections between observational terms. These empirical associations are hypothetical merely because the observations included have not yet been tested systematically. The experimenter may make a positive hypothesis, which in turn implies a null hypothesis to be tested; if the null hypothesis is rejected, the positive hypothesis is supposedly confirmed. Aside from the problem that disconfirming the null hypothesis does not confirm a positive hypothesis, prior expression of a positive hypothetical generalization is redundant because it is already implied in the design. To the empiricist, rejection of a null hypothesis is equivalent to confirmation of a positive hypothesis. Radical empiricist methodologists, such as Sidman, claim on the other hand that positive hypotheses should not be stated ahead of time, simply because one will be more likely to see the unexpected if one has no preconception of what is to be found. He apparently believes that one major purpose of research is to find

[6] Murray Sidman, *Tactics of Scientific Research* (New York: Basic Books, Inc., 1960), p. 15.

"serendipitous" patterns in the data. Unfortunately, this approach is somewhat futile if the positive hypotheses are already implied in the experimental design. It means no more than that the researcher can claim after his research is completed that he has made some significant "discoveries," those discoveries having been made simply by sorting out the cases in which the null hypothesis was rejected. Moreover, although this procedure is an excuse for setting up an unstructured set of variables for testing, that unstructured research content still implies a full set of positive hypotheses consisting of the association of all variables tested.

"Theory" is often introduced into the research design by selecting from among the works of so-called theorists and introducing their attempts to describe society as if they were scientific theories. *The American Soldier,* for example, was supposed to have incorporated the theoretical writings of Vilfredo Pareto, Thomas, and George Herbert Mead.[7] This procedure not only provides the researcher with a feeling that he has actually used theory in his design (especially if the "theorist" chosen did no data collection himself), but also solves the problem of selecting from among the great diversity of perceptions of things something which may be thought to be important. Borrowing empirical categories of Mead, Thomas, and Pareto easily provides criteria for selection. The importance of the "theorist" and the high esteem given to him are reasons enough for use of his ideas because then the experiment itself is backed by the method of *authority*. This is a partial explanation of the symbolic relationship between empirical research and grand theory in sociology. If the researcher can borrow his hypothetical empirical generalizations ("theories") and empirical categories ("concepts"), the whole procedure of experimentation becomes automatic, and no thought is required at all.

The simplest experimental design includes an "experimental" and a "control" group of subjects. These are made similar to each other in composition by means of "matching" to ensure the sharing of important characteristics and/or by random selection to ensure that neither group is more likely to have more of some possible confounding characteristics. Next the experimental group is sub-

[7] See Stouffer, *The American Soldier,* p. 33.

jected to a manipulation (sometimes called a "treatment" or a "cause") while the control group is left alone. Then some characteristic of the groups is observed and recorded, usually by the administration of a psychological scaling procedure of some sort. For example, in *The American Soldier* study enlisted men were shown propaganda films and then asked how much they would like to kill (in terms of response categories scaled according to the strength of the desire to kill). Occasionally a pretest is given to determine whether the two groups were actually similar at the outset according to the dependent variable tested. Actually the pretest is not a logical necessity if one considers either matching or randomization sufficient to ensure the equivalence of the experimental and control groups. In the case of the soldiers a pretest was given to gain more assurance that the urge to kill the "enemy" was indeed increased by the propaganda. Pretests have the difficulty that the group may not react to the manipulation "naturally" the next time through. This is solved by generating more groups (both experimental and control) which are given no pretest, and statistically comparing the results of all.

The idea of experimental and control groups tested for differences follows Mill's canon of difference. When interpreted according to Mill's scheme, the design results in a relation of sufficiency, the cause (manipulation) producing the effect (result of the scaling procedure). But it does not establish necessity, that this cause alone can produce this effect. This would require the inclusion of a method of agreement, but the Fisher design works for differences only. The point that necessity is not entailed in the design is ignored, and findings are reported as if their relation were both necessary and sufficient; however, the idea of multiple causation provides a legitimization for ignoring necessity through the assumption that a multiplicity of causes can produce the same effect. This curious legitimization may have its source in the bureaucratic settings in which much sociological research takes place. Most bureaucratic purposes may be served equally well by a number of findings. In the study of soldiers, for example, the generals wanted their soldiers to be ready to kill and did not care how they were prepared as long as preparation was effective. If films worked, that was good enough. The job of the sociologist–bureaucrat was to see if the propaganda films worked at all and, if so, how well. It was not practical to support a number of further studies intended to prove that that method alone would work. The only important point was that it did work. This conception of causative science neatly fits the empiricist conception of science, a conception which results in a body of knowledge to be used to facilitate effective action (and thus consolidate or support power positions).

Experimental designs of greater complexity are used in empiricist sociology, but most are merely elaborations of the simpler design. All of them are concerned with making observational associations between observational categories. These associations are all made by rejecting the null hypothesis and jumping to the opposed hypothesis based on some sort of manipulation. If desired, a level of relationship can be ascribed to the association by means of one or another correlational procedure. Indeed, the whole procedure might be described as systematic magic, for it is similar to the use of magic by primitives in nearly every respect, except the conviction by its practitioners that they can eventually discover what is "really there" and have true scientific knowledge. The primitive also thinks that the results of his routinized procedures will produce certain effects and that past empirical associations will hold in the future, but he believes that he is caught in a web of contending unobserved causes which may foul up his results. Both types of magic rigorously follow procedures of association; both involve mechanical processes which, if followed closely, never require reflective thought; both are concerned with the production of effects, but only the modern systematic magician is self-consciously empiricistic in the face of alternative ways of making connections in thought.

The problem of induction of findings beyond the limits of the laboratory experiment is compounded by the artificiality of conditions introduced to gain power of manipulation and control when faced with potentially "confounding causes" in a universe of multiple causation. This artificiality means that the conditions under which the experiment took place are not similar to natural cases, and, since the basis of induction is through similarity, the ability to induce to natural cases is lost. In other conditions in which induction is applied, it proceeds from a random sample of which we have knowledge to the population from which it was drawn. This procedure is based on the assumed similarity of the sample to the population. But randomization of selection of subjects for the experiment does not make the conditions under which it is carried out any less artificial as compared with conditions outside the lab. Empiricist inductions based on similarity thus cannot be carried out. No generalizations can be made outside the lab itself. In other words, studying a sample randomly drawn from a population under conditions unlike any others found in the experience of that population (as in an empirically controlled lab experiment) means not that the results can be induced back to the population, but only that if others from the same population were brought into the lab their responses to experimental conditions would be unlikely to be different from those of the sample.

Artificiality in the empiricist lab experiment is unlike artificiality in science, which comes from abstractive and rational connection. The scope of a scientific law determines the empirical circumstances which may be handled by it including some conditions which may be approximated in the lab. Here both natural and lab circumstances are abstractively related to the definitional scope of the law. The scope of application is entailed in the law and is not based on control of conditions by the empirical processes of matching or randomization. The circumstances under which a law holds perfectly are not open to empirical generalization. We do not have vacuums and frictionless surfaces in nature. Therefore, although scientific experiments may be said to be "artificial" in the sense that they are not descriptive of typical or average empirical conditions, they are unlike the conditions of empirical artificiality found in empiricist lab experiments. The scientist is not, in fact, *inducing* from lab experiments at all. The law may be *used* in the lab if its conditions of application are approximated, but it is not developed there. The purpose of introducing artificiality into the scientific experiment is different from that of artificiality in empiricist experiments. In science, artificiality is a consequence of the use of a rational law in empirical circumstances, but the empiricist is attempting to sort out pure cause–effect relations from the web of natural causes and effects.

In science no attempt is made to induce from experiments; but, although induction is the purpose of empiricist experiments, there is no basis for it in their procedures. According to Leon Festinger, "the laboratory experiment should be an attempt to create a situation in which the operation of variables will be clearly seen under special identified and defined conditions. It matters not whether such a situation would ever be encountered in real life." [8] This statement would be accurate if he were referring to scientific experiments, but his examples make it clear that he was not. Artificiality is indeed a necessary characteristic of empiricist lab experiments in which an effort is made to control all but a few (usually all but one) influences (independent variables) on the result (dependent variable) to determine whether there is an empirical association and, if so, the level of relatedness. If such a pure causal association is made, the problem remains that it must be fit back into the natural web of confused causes from which it was taken if it is to be used in a causal explanation. The empiricist occasionally voices a hope that if one gathered enough such findings (for example, all findings imaginable that might be related to "small group behavior") about similar observables, the total web of causal relations might fall into place, and he could then apply his findings to natural cases. Unfortunately, the problem of the lack of universality of causal associations renders this hope futile.

The apparent solution to the empiricist problem of artificiality and its curtailment of induction is the field experiment which actually more closely approximates the spirit of Fisher's work. Fisher's experiments were literally field experiments using agricultural fields. Field experiments in sociology differ from laboratory experiments in that they take place in natural circumstances and are concerned with natural groups such as boys' friendship groups or labor unions. Almost any subordinate group can be the subject of a field experiment. (The empiricists have found that they do not have the power to study such groups as the president's cabinet, the American Medical Association, or top manufacturing executives. Such groups are reluctant to submit themselves to sociological manipulation.) The field experiment differs from a survey in that there is an experimental group which is actually subject to manipulation, often some

[8] Leon Festinger, "Laboratory Experiments," in Leon Festinger and Daniel Katz, eds., *Research Methods in the Behavioral Sciences* (New York: The Dryden Press, 1953), p. 139.

sort of planned change imposed on a group of subordinates, such as speeding up the work process on an assembly line. The role of the empiricist can be to determine the effects on their attitudes.

The statistical design of the field experiment is identical to that of the lab experiment. Because of the lack of the problem of artificiality in the field, because groups such as assembly lines do share at least a few similar superficial characteristics if only because they are all engaged in the production of goods for profit, it is believed that induction to other natural cases is justified. Studies of planned change of one assembly line should be relevant to other assembly lines if the differences between the unique human beings concerned can be ignored.

Elimination of the problem of artificiality often means that some power of control has been lost. While the planned change on the assembly line was being carried out many other things were happening in the lives of the workers which might interfere with clear determination of real causes. To the empiricist these things may also be confounding factors, possible causes of the differences to be observed in the attitudes between his experimental and control groups or differences in the groups themselves from one time to another. His confidence in the association itself is less than that of the empiricist laboratory experimenter. Thus, the uncertain associations established in field experiments lack the rigor of associations established in the lab. The loss of artificiality through controls means the loss of a method of sorting causes from the causal web. The rejection of a null hypothesis actually leaves no basis for a feeling of confidence that any particular positive hypothesis is right. Uncontrolled confounding causes may confound the experimenter himself, for he does not know whether to affirm his favored hypothesis, to affirm all possible confounding causes, or to affirm some hypothesis including both his selected causal variable and all possible confounding causes. When total control is not possible, field experiments are unrigorously uncertain. Furthermore, when in an attempt to keep conditions natural, the empiricist does not randomly assign or match groups but uses naturally occurring groups, the test of significance is meaningless, and no association whatsoever can be established.

Some empiricists have outlined a gradation of types of experiments from lab to field experiments. These types have little significance here, for they are simply concerned with the trading off of power of control against lessened artificiality. In fact, empiricist experimenters in sociology are caught in a dilemma. If they use controls in the lab their conditions are too artificial and dissimilar from natural cases to make inductions to them; but when natural cases are used in the field the level of control of confounding factors is usually so low that no single positive hypothesis can be posited after rejecting the null hypothesis, and there is consequently nothing to induce from. The argument that this dilemma can be resolved by using first one method and then the other collapses immediately when given a minimum of thought. If there is no similarity of conditions, there is no basis for induction from one setting to the other. Results from experiments in natural cases can no more be induced to the lab than can results from the lab be induced to natural cases. On the other hand, if a positive empirical hypothesis were posited a priori broad enough to include both the artificial conditions of the lab and natural conditions (not that this is even possible, because the use of controls in the lab is in a sense a negation of the uncontrolled natural situation), the resulting generalization would be so vague that it would be practically meaningless. For example, although we may claim, after having carried out both a lab and a field experiment, that "people like better groups that are harder to get into," there is still no sense in which the experimental situations were similar. Therefore, they still cannot be added up to a single general statement. The empiricist may say that "the people in my lab experiment mostly preferred groups that were harder to get into" and "the people in my field experiment mostly preferred groups that were harder to get into," but this does not add up to the universal generalization "people prefer groups that are harder to get into." The lab experiment results can be induced to nothing except other similarly conditioned lab experiments using people from the same population (even ignoring the fact that population is bound by time and space and will not be the same at any other time than the time at which the experimental groups were originally chosen), and the field experiment results can be induced to nothing but the transient population from which the sample was originally drawn. In fact, all the empiricist can say is, "A few people that I studied under such and such conditions prefer groups that are harder to get into."

It might be claimed that if controls were introduced in the field, associations and inductions could be made, but the conditions of power required to obtain such a level of control exist only in total institutions such as the army, asylums, and prisons. The inmates of these institutions are nearly powerless as a consequence of the elaborate means of social control already imposed. The empiricist, working in cooperation with the appropriate administrators and generals, has under these conditions the ability to use controls in "natural" situations comparable to the rigor of the lab. This attempt to resolve the dilemma was first extensively used by sociological empiricists in the study of *The American Soldier.* Nevertheless, a problem of scope remains: inductions cannot be made to any natural situation in which repressive controls do not exist. The results, in fact, can be useful only to the administrators of such institutions because only there are *similar* conditions to be found. Where individuals are free from such control, the conditions of the experiment are negated.

Thus, only in conditions of enslavement of some people by others can the results of such experiments be used. Perhaps we can set up more efficient concentration camps, but we cannot add to the useful knowledge of free men. No matter how dimly perceived these uses are, they call into question the aims of the support of empiricist social experiments by government and business. In fact, empiricist knowledge is not scientific and exists solely to implement effective action; when this knowledge is called into use in particular empirical situations in society (when it is knowledge about people), it can only be used by those people with power and knowledge against those without them, thus making the actions of the powerful more effective. Empiricist racial experiments can be of use in causing people to do things against their will. The more people are in fact controlled, the more this knowledge can be used to implement greater control in a cumulative process. It should, of course, be understood that the empiricist sociologist is an unwitting contributor to this process. He is not himself a powerholder—he is "value neutral." Yet a totalitarian state provides the best conditions for the use of the results of experimental empiricist sociology.

Critiques by "radical sociologists" of establishment sociologists funded by government and business to conduct empiricist studies make sense in this context. These critiques accurately claim that the results of establishment sociology are inherently biased in that they can be used only by those who have power over others. But the radicals are wrong in attributing this to science. In fact, the radicals have not contested the false claim of establishment sociologists that they are collecting scientific knowledge. *Scientific* social science, however, has very different implications.

The Survey

As in the empiricist experiment, the purpose of the modern sociological survey is not simply to gather facts through sampling procedures but to systematically establish relationships by empirical generalization. Modern sociologists tend to be involved with gathering facts about such groups as the poor and the working classes. Surveys have been done by large bureaucratic states for hundreds of years to facilitate the gathering of taxes and the administration of affairs of state. Yet the modern sociological survey, as a unique form, is no older than *The American Soldier*. Stouffer, who directed that study, maintained that controlled experimentation is the only certain way to demonstrate that *A* causes *B*.[9] However, proof based on the model of the controlled experiment is difficult to achieve with social data,[10] so it may in practice be necessary to *deviate* from the "ideal model."

Stouffer explains the ideal model of controlled experimentation (claiming that it originates from the design of experiments in psychology and the practices of physical scientists while ignoring the crucial contribution of Fisher) by in fact presenting Fisher's model as represented in Figure 6. Stouffer explained that the two groups should be matched and differentiated only by the "stimulus" which is applied only to the experimental group. The *X*s refer to the

[9] See Stouffer, *The American Soldier,* p. 16.

[10] See Stouffer, "Some Observations on Study Design," *American Journal of Sociology,* Vol. 55, June 1950, p. 355. See also Stouffer, *The American Soldier,* pp. 48–49.

	Before	After	
Experimental group	X_1	X_2	$d = X_2 - X_1$
Control group	X'_1	X'_2	$d' = X'_2 - X'_1$

FIGURE 6. Stouffer's ideal model of controlled experimentation

results of pre- and post-tests, and Stouffer interpreted the statistical test as a test of whether the $d - d'$ difference is likely to be greater than that expected by chance. According to Stouffer, then, the only difference between the ideal experiment and the survey is that the survey does not produce data to fill all four boxes. This reduces the differences between surveys and experiments simply to a difference between amounts of data collected. What is left to the survey (in this case a panel study of two surveys taken at different times on the same group) is illustrated in Figure 7. In this design there is a time lapse, but there is only one group and the test of significance can therefore be applied only to the differences observed in the group over time. The most common survey design, however, was

Before	After	
X_1	X_2	$d = X_2 - X_1$

FIGURE 7. The design of a survey for one group over time

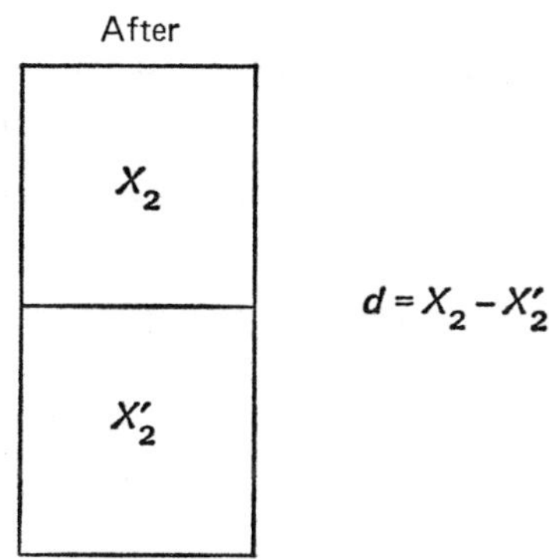

FIGURE 8. The design of a survey for two groups

illustrated by Stouffer as in Figure 8. Here two groups (for example, whites and blacks or rural and urban dwellers) are compared at a single point in time according to the statistical data (X_2 and X_2') derived from some scaling procedure, and the difference (d) is tested statistically. In neither of these cases are there as many data as there would have been in the ideal controlled experiment, and they therefore are not as satisfactory. According to Stouffer, particular surveys can be viewed as "ingenious approximations" of experiments.[11]

The results of one such ingenious approximation done by Stouffer's group are represented in Figure 9. In that study, the attitudes toward racial mixing of white enlisted men from divisions having no black platoons were compared with attitudes of men from divisions which had black platoons. In the mixed division (the "experimental" group) only 7 percent said they "disliked" the idea of racial mixing, while 62 percent of the unmixed (control) group "disliked" it.[12] Obviously Stouffer thought of the mixing as an experimental stimulus. Because of the empty "before" boxes, however, there may be some doubt about whether the difference in response found was due to the "stimulus," but Stouffer had two

[11] Stouffer, "Some Afterthoughts of a Contributor to *The American Soldier*," in Robert K. Merton and Paul F. Lazarsfeld, eds., *Continuities in Social Research* (New York: The Free Press, 1950), p. 211.

[12] See Stouffer, "Some Observations on Study Design," p. 358.

	Before	After
Experimental		7%
Control		62%

FIGURE 9. Comparison of attitudes of soldiers toward racial mixing

justifications for his inference. First, because both groups had about the same proportion of Southerners, he inferred that their earlier attitudes were similar. Hence if the two groups were matched on one or more significant characteristics, their similarity would have been even greater, and the inference about the effect of the stimulus would be even more certain. Today this is a common feature of survey analysis. The second basis for Stouffer's inference was the fact that the enlisted men in the experimental group were asked to *recall* their attitudes before the mixing, and 67 percent said that they remembered being opposed. He consequently believed his "proof" to be almost as strong as that of the ideal experiment.

From Stouffer's point of view, the experiment and the survey differ not in kind but in the amount of data available. The difference between the two designs is only that the survey does not fill all of the boxes with data. The analysis may, nevertheless, be undertaken by "ingenious" people capable of working in the absence of the missing data or of making inferences from the available data to fill the empty boxes. The results of survey work are still tentative in comparison with the experiment, but Stouffer attributed this to the youth of the science in which "exploratory research is of necessity fumbling."[13] Less rigorous designs may be tolerated in less-

[13] *Ibid.*, p. 360.

well-developed science. P. L. Kendall and Paul F. Lazarsfeld claim that sociological thought is rarely advanced enough to start out with "sharply formulated hypotheses" and that exploratory studies are needed to provide the knowledge upon which to base such hypotheses.[14] Of course, the absence of "sharply formulated hypotheses" prior to research is not a consequence of the alleged youth of sociology but of its empiricism. An absence of a rational system from which to derive determinative hypotheses means that the a priori hypotheses will be made assuming that empirical generalizations are theory. Such generalizations are necessarily vague.

This treatment of the survey as if it were an experiment with less data to fill the boxes is the legitimization used for combining the techniques of public opinion polling developed by Gallup, Crossler, and Roper with Fisher's design for agricultural experimentation, Pearson's correlational procedures, and a dash of Mill. The finished mess is passed off as a legitimized method for conducting scientific surveys. In fact, with a little seasoning it has been transformed into a fixed procedure.

The survey is supposedly made similar to the experiment by the process of elaboration as described by Lazarsfeld and Kendall and used in *The American Soldier* as well as a great number of later studies. Kendall and Lazarsfeld agree that the ideal way to study cause–effect relations is by experiment; but, because of the "difficulty" of conducting such experiments, they propose the use of "approximations provided by survey materials." [15] Survey analysis is concerned with the "clarification" of statistical relationships between two or more variables. Kendall and Lazarsfeld claim that statistical relationships imply causal connections, whether or not causality is explicitly asserted. The purpose of statistical analysis of survey data is to uncover these causal connections in a manner very similar to Mill's methods of sorting out the real causal regularities from the totality of causal relations in a regular universe. Elaboration, like Mill's canons, is intended to "uncover" these "underlying regularities."

The completed survey provides a multitude of scale values for

[14] See P. L. Kendall and Paul F. Lazarsfeld, "Problems of Survey Analysis," in Merton and Lazarsfeld; *Continuities in Social Research,* p. 133.

[15] *Ibid.,* p. 136.

those who were surveyed, which are subsequently tested for association and related by correlational procedures. The data form a microcosmic Mill-type universe, and the problem of the researcher is to juggle around all the possible relations among his data until the "real regularities" are sorted out. The sociological survey researcher is, however, faced with an easier task than the empiricist simply using Mill's canons, for the universe of the former at least consists of a denumerable quantity of observations while the latter has to cope with the whole universe. But this simplification of the sorting procedure by closing off some of the larger universe means that all possible data were not gathered and some possible relations will not be discovered while some variables crucial to control will not be available. Almost every survey report mentions these problems. The initial decision as to the area to be encompassed by the survey immediately limits the data gathered, and this limitation makes elaboration possible.

Elaboration is concerned with a process of interpretation in which the survey researcher attempts to relate what he thinks is a cause to what he thinks is its effect through the introduction of various "controls," "intervening variables," and other expedients into the survey itself. Kendall and Lazarsfeld analyzed the finding that 68 percent of a group of comparatively well educated draftees were hostile to having been drafted compared with a 78 percent hostility from a less educated group of draftees. This statistical finding was transformed into a statement of "causal relation" through the following elaboration: Joining the army involves a deprivation. To decide which group felt more greatly deprived it is necessary to discover what reference group they relate themselves to. In this case the reference group of the less educated is likely to be the working class, and that of the more educated is likely to be the middle class. Because the working class received more deferments than the middle class, the less educated probably felt greater deprivation relative to the probable reference group. Thus, we are supposed to infer that reference groups cause differences in hostility.

In another example of elaboration offered by Morris Rosenberg we are presented with the finding that working classes are more likely to vote Democratic than middle classes. The first question is whether the relationship is to be considered real or only apparent.

Extraneous variables such as religion are considered at this point. Because middle classes are found to be more likely to be Protestant and Protestants are more likely to vote Republican, we divide the classes into Protestants and non-Protestants and check whether the relationship between social class and voting still holds in each subsample. We may similarly divide the sample into subsamples based on geographic area of residence based on the finding that Southerners are more likely to vote Democratic. To make sure that our final causal connection is not messed up by extraneous variables the separation of religious characteristics should be maintained so that both are controlled at once. We might also include a separation by age, as older groups are no longer upwardly mobile.

The method of elaboration cannot escape from the basic problem inherent in the empirical attempt to establish causal relations. Although here the attempt is being made to establish probable instead of invariant relations, either of the examples should be elaborated to include controls for almost any observable characteristic of the members of the population since arguments can be made in favor of including, for example, such observables as sex, race, number of children, marital status, and type of occupation in the determination of choice of political parties.

The example of elaboration taken from Lazarsfeld and Kendall was intended to *explain* a relationship, but Rosenberg's elaboration introduced additional variables to illustrate a further use of elaboration as a device for checking whether a relationship is sound. In the latter case, the use of an intervening variable such as an attitude (liberalism) between the association of class position and voting preference (Democratic) can be used to make the causal chain more plausible. Alternatively we might search for "suppressed" variables (and remove Jews, who are likely to be both more wealthy and more Democratic) to see if this has an effect on the strength of the relationship. This type of thinking follows the spirit of Mill and is not without the associated problems.

Most surveys are administered at a single point in time and thus have no time dimension.[16] But the idea of a causal relationship includes the assumption that a cause is followed in time by an effect,

[16] Some surveys are administered at two different time periods.

and for such surveys no causal relationship can be established. (Furthermore, the statistical procedures used, unlike the cause–effect relation, are not directional.) Two "ingenious" solutions to this problem have been offered. The first is to introduce the retrospective question such as, "How did you feel about integrated divisions before Negro platoons were introduced?" It may be acceptable to include the responses to such questions as data of a sort, but to infer that they have something to do with the actual prior mental state of the soldiers before their divisions were integrated it would be necessary to have given them a questionnaire previously and to have compared their responses to their remembered attitudes at the later date. In other words, data are necessary. The second solution is concerned with the supposed inherent logical character of the observational categories themselves. Rosenberg gives the following example: "If Negroes are more alienated than whites, it is evident that the alienation cannot be responsibile for the race." [17] This may appear obvious, but it ignores the fact that the category "Negro" is socially defined. If in the United States some members of society are separated out, alienated from another group, and called "Negro," then one could conclude, on the contrary, that being alienated causes the status "Negro" and any psychological manifestations found by the empiricist in his survey. Simply because an observational characteristic appears superficially to be an obviously inherent characteristic of an individual (such as skin color, hair color, or age) and thus seems to be a given cause of attitudes and not an effect, we cannot conclude that the time dimension problem has been solved because the separation of those characteristics into observable categories, and their significance to society, are themselves based on attitudes.

Because the two standard methods of establishing asymmetry are so full of logical holes, this approach to survey research is not an appropriate technique for establishing causal relations unless the meaning of "causal relations" is drastically altered. The survey researcher is left, therefore, with the alternative of working simply with an interpretation of the statistical relations themselves. In this case, the symmetry of significance tests and measures of relatedness

[17] Morris Rosenberg, *The Logic of Survey Analysis* (New York: Basic Books, Inc.), p. 12.

means that one can ignore the problem of which variable came first.

The problem of establishing causal relations is, in fact, only a minor one in comparison with the other problems facing the survey researcher. More crucial is the fact that the design of survey research itself will not support the establishment of associations by statistical means. The typical empiricist survey researcher is accustomed to thinking of survey research in Stouffer's terms, as an experiment with some data missing. But Stouffer was wrong; the survey is not like the empiricist experiment, and the use of significance tests is illegitimate. The survey researcher draws a random sample from a population to provide a basis for inference from the sample to the population; but this is the only use of randomization, and it is concerned exclusively with that inductive process and not at all with the problem of establishing association in the sample. In contrast, the experimental and control groups in empiricist experiments are created by random assignment in an attempt to ensure that the two groups are identical before the manipulation. *The test of significance is based on the inclusion of these two similar groups and its distribution is based on the random assignment of individuals to them.* The null hypothesis can be stated only because these two groups can be assumed to be similar within the limits of chance. But logically the design of surveys is completely different, and tests of significance are not appropriate to them.

In the survey the random assignment of individuals to experimental and control groups has been replaced by empirical categories such as upper class and lower class. The objects contained in these categories (such as upper- and lower-class people) were not assigned randomly and cannot therefore be said to be similar at any point in time. Neither category was manipulated. They differ in as many characteristics as we wish to observe. Because there is no random distribution between these two categories, it is not particularly intelligent to use a significance test based on the assumption of random distribution. The test of significance calculated for categories, such as upper or lower class, rural or urban, black or white skin, simply has no meaning as a test of association. Statistically, the between-group variations are supposed to be due to the operation of chance; but if the two groups were not randomly assigned (for example, the assumption would have to be that individuals might have been randomly assigned a skin color), then one cannot ask whether the difference is due to chance. Because we know that the difference is *not* due to chance, the null hypothesis and test of significance are meaningless. But empiricists insist on mechanically calculating significance in spite of the fact that significance cannot be interpreted for such data.

Even worse, although no inference can be made about deviation of the differences of empiricist survey categories from chance (meaning that no null hypothesis can be constructed), the empiricist then insists on asserting positive hypotheses.[18] Clearly such an assertion is preposterous. The empiricist attempting to prove that social class and voting patterns are associated might run his survey data through the statistical test and conclude from the result that it is unlikely that the association of the data is due to chance. Aside from the fact that the procedure up to this point is meaningless, if the individuals of the different social classes were alike in all respects but social class (just as experimental and control groups are alike in all respects but manipulation), then it might be possible to make the positive inference that there was an association between social class and voting. But upper- and lower-class individuals differ in numerous characteristics besides the one observed. They differ in amount of education, church attendance, length of working day, number of cars per family, length of vacations, attendance of meetings, place of residence, value of clothing, number of children, number of dogs, number of swimming pools, religious affiliation, and so forth. With which of these is voting behavior really associated? These differences and many more are possible; therefore, no single positive inference may be hypothesized from the rejection of the null hypothesis. To do that, all possible asso-

[18] When certain empiricists think that they perceive less than perfect associations between two survey research categories, they argue that there are sampling and measurement errors. They then mistake random errors for random assignment of individuals to groups, as in the Fisher design of experiments. Even if such random errors were real, they would not logically be like randomness of assignment to groups and would not provide a basis for positing a null hypothesis. More fundamentally, the information from data does not provide an association but a set of categories with a certain number of people in each category. Both the supposed association and the random errors exist only in the mind of the empiricist.

ciations must be checked, and that is not possible. This situation is logically different from the ideal empiricist experiment in which the two groups have been assigned randomly so that they may be assumed to be initially alike in all respects.

The method of elaboration attempts to solve this problem by matching upper-class and lower-class groups according to all "important" characteristics which differ between them. This procedure works on the assumption that the researcher is able to sort out and observe all possible relevant alternative hypotheses and thus control for them to discover the "real" association. This makes the association itself completely dependent on the ability of the researcher to observe accurately and completely. It turns the procedure of finding an objective real association into a completely *subjective* process. The result is one subjectively selected association sorted out from an objectively unlimited universe. The number of associations found is thus limited only by the number of researchers. This problem is obscured in the empiricist research procedure either by standardizing survey procedures in such a way that particular measuring instruments (questionnaires) are used time after time so that the "important" variables become a matter of tradition or by including an elaborate set of empirical generalizations ("hypotheses") which are vague enough (not having theoretical definitions) that they can be used to justify a multitude of empirical studies. In the latter case, a so-called theory is used to determine what associations are real, and (because the test of significance is not a legitimate basis for establishing association) the belief in the accuracy of the associations is completely dependent on the "authority" or "significance" of the "theorists." The significance of the theorist is, in turn, related to the number of researchers who have used his work, and we may again observe the elaborate ritual of mutual back-scratching which supports empiricist sociology when its logic fails.

Hanan C. Selvin has argued that the conditions under which the test of significance should be used are almost impossible to reach in survey research.[19] In other words, being urban or rural, as this does not involve random assignment, necessarily entails what he

[19] See Hanan C. Selvin, "A Critique of Tests of Significance in Survey Research," *American Sociological Review*, Vol. 22, October 1957, p. 520.

calls "correlated biases." Correlated biases refer to those additional characteristics of the people in the two groups which are also related to the other tested variable (political interest, for example) along with the characteristic used for their original separation (such as rural and urban). For example, because urban families are smaller, urban parents may have more leisure time which may be related to an interest in politics. Therefore, one should control for family size if one wishes to know the effect urban or rural location alone has on an interest in politics. Selvin points out that unless we know that the effect of the correlated biases is less than the effect of random variations, it is senseless to test for randomness: "Under these conditions to ask whether the observed difference could have been produced by random errors is like wondering whether one's car has stopped because of random misbehavior of the electrons in the ignition system without first making sure there is gasoline in the tank." [20] Selvin therefore concludes that "only when all important correlated biases have been controlled is it legitimate to measure the possible influence of random errors by statistical tests of significance." [21] As in practice it is always impossible to control that effectively, Selvin's argument amounts to an assertion that tests of significance should never be used on survey data. Furthermore, since the test of significance is a test for random distribution and *not* (as Selvin claimed) *a test of random errors,* its use makes no sense at all in this context.

Robert McGinnis's disagreement with Selvin is based on the fear that social scientists will suffer a "business slump" if they allow themselves to be diverted from their profits by logical argument. He recognizes that Selvin's argument leads to the conclusion that the whole basis of legitimization of determining association from surveys must be rejected and consequently chooses to reject the argument to save the procedure. To avoid the problem that "most social researchers would soon be out of business" [22] if Selvin's logic were accepted, he argues, for example, that although it is important to know that measured differences in intelligence between races

[20] *Ibid.,* p. 522.

[21] *Ibid.*

[22] Robert McGinnis, "Randomization and Inference in Sociological Research," *American Sociological Review,* Vol. 23, August 1958, p. 413.

disappear when proper controls are used, it is still important to know if there are measured differences in intelligence between the races.[23] Furthermore, he argues that the lack of random assignment of individuals to categories (such as rural and urban) does not violate the statistical assumptions of the test of significance.[24] Here his argument seems to be supported only by authority. The only real problem, then, as he sees it, is that of interpretation, which he claims is partially solved by the use of some controls. He criticizes Selvin for seemingly desiring to obtain universal knowledge from the survey method. McGinnis asserts, on the contrary, that "there is no such thing as a completely general relationship which is independent of population, time and space." [25] Certainly this statement is true for the results of empiricist methods, but it is obviously false for scientific knowledge, because a defining characteristic of a law is nonlimited scope.

McGinnis's assumption that uncontrolled hypotheses are of utility in prediction contradicts his claim that general relationships are population-bound. If populations include time in their frame, then any general relationship derived from empirical study of it refers only to the past and thus has no predictive value. McGinnis may have diverted social science from a business slump, but he has contributed strongly to the empiricist intellectual slump.

The empirical methods of social science have been so routinized that we often lose sight of the intended logic behind them. Empiricists seem blissfully unaware that Fisher's method of arriving at rigorously uncertain associations is unworkable unless it is controlled by an already existing scientific law, and they do not know that his method cannot legitimately be applied to survey research data because it is unlike the experiment. Statistical generalizations from survey research are unrigorously uncertain. No positive associations can be made in the survey, and thus it is meaningless to relate variables by correlation.

Compared with the empiricist experiment, however, the survey method provides a better basis for induction. Here (at least if proper procedures of attaining a random sample are followed) we

[23] *Ibid.*, p. 413.

[24] *Ibid.*

[25] *Ibid.*, p. 412.

may induce from the sample to the population from which it was drawn if we are willing to assume that on the average the sample is like the population. In survey research, at least, the sample is not artificially separated from the population. Nevertheless, as McGinnis pointed out, these inductions are limited to the unique population from which the sample was drawn. Therefore, no universal statements and no predictions can be made. The findings from a survey of the poor in New York City in 1970 are not necessarily relevant to the poor in New York City in 1971. The result of the inductions from survey work are not general statements but merely particulars for a group larger than the sample.

Survey findings, given the time lapse between study and publication, consist of nothing but knowledge about the past. They are not only nonpredictive but are not even relevant to existing circumstances. The utility of surveys (if any) is descriptive and historical. General relationships cannot be established; but, instead of rejecting the value of surveys as a scientific technique, this inadequacy has only led to more and more surveys. Not realizing that the problem is inherent in the technique itself, survey researchers attribute it to the fact that all the facts are not yet in, and this leads them to conclude that continuous fact gathering is necessary. Indeed, it is a logical impossibility for all the facts to be in until doomsday, and then there will be no survey researchers to collect them.

The survey results in relative frequencies and nothing more. The attempt to transform these frequencies into empirical relationships by the application of statistical procedures is unjustified and futile. It is bad empiricism and even worse science. Because the procedure of generating apparent empirical relations is so dependent on the arbitrary selection of so-called controls, the survey analyst has to supplement his procedures with his common sense, which is simply culturally-determined empiricism and therefore also arbitrary. Science, on the other hand, rejects the use of common sense in favor of rational and abstractive thought. This allows the structuring of theories which are universal, related determinatively, and may therefore be used to explain particulars. Survey research, limited to studying the relative reality of particulars, cannot transcend them, cannot generalize, and therefore cannot explain or predict.

The justification for survey research lies in the desire for individuals or groups who can support it to gather information (usually about other groups) which can be used for their own advantage. Since the lower classes do not often possess the funds to support such research, they are seldom able to tap this important source of information. A glance at surveys produced from the time of *The American Soldier* to the present will verify that these studies are typically characterized by a power-related bias. The empiricist sociologist enters the picture as a powerless bureaucrat who takes no responsibility for the uses to which his work is put because he feels that he is contributing to the progress of social science. The survey researcher, however, is doing neither science nor even good empiricism and is no more than a tool for those who have the power to purchase his services.

Empiricism offers no basis for selection of topics for study among the infinity of things which can be observed, but funded research offers a convenient solution allowing "authorities" of the organization supporting the research to determine its content by the selection of studies to be funded. The survey researcher is therefore often no more than a well-trained spy for those having the economic power to support him.

5 causality

The methodological problems of systematic empiricism in sociology are so numerous that new techniques for "research" such as Hubert Blalock's techniques for causal inference are enthusiastically welcomed in the hope that the field will thereby rest on firmer ground. Blalock's technique for analysis of survey data is somewhat different from (and was hoped to be better than) the older one developed by Paul Lazarsfeld. Like Lazarsfeld, Blalock tries to sort out causal relations through the use of empirical controls. He chooses to begin with survey data because the survey is in his opinion the most important sociological method. He concentrates on continuous variables (such as a range of income) rather than on categorized data (such as low, middle, and high incomes). His book *Causal Inferences in Nonexperimental Research* is primarily concerned with interpreting path analysis using the partial correlation technique (a post factum analytic statistical technique).

According to J. P. Guilford, "A partial correlation between two things is one that nullifies the effects of a third variable."[1] Since

[1] J. P. Guilford, *Fundamental Statistics in Psychology and Education* (New York: McGraw-Hill Book Company, 1956), p. 316.

correlations do not necessarily indicate cause–effect relations, the interpretation of "nullifies the effects" requires explanation. Clearly, partial correlation is not an experimental technique; therefore, "nullifies the effects" is not equivalent to "experimentally holds constant." Instead the statistician treats "nullifies the effects" as if it is definitionally equivalent to the following equation:

$$r_{12.3} = \frac{r_{12} - r_{13}r_{23}}{\sqrt{(1 - r_{13}^2)(1 - r_{23}^2)}}$$

in which r_{12}, r_{13}, and r_{23} are correlational values and $r_{12.3}$ is the value of the relation between 1 and 2 with the influence of 3 on 1 and on 2 removed. The intended meaning of the equation becomes clear from examination of the numerator on the left side. For example, when the product of r_{13} and r_{23} is equal to r_{12} the numerator is zero, and the value of $r_{12.3}$ is consequently zero. It is therefore concluded that there is no $1 \rightarrow 2$ relationship independent of the influence of 3. Examples between these extremes supposedly make at least as much sense.

Guilford explains partial correlations with an example in which the correlation of height and weight for a group of boys in an age group from 12 to 19 (r_{12}) was .78, the correlation of height and age (r_{13}) was .52, and of weight and age (r_{23}) was .54. Plugging this into the equation for partial equations, we get

$$r_{12.3} = \frac{.78 - (.52 \times .54)}{(1 - .52^2)(1 - .54^2)} = .69$$

or a correlation figure for height and weight with age held constant. Given a fourth variate (strength, perhaps) a second order partial correlation would be calculated by an analogous equation:

$$r_{12.34} = \frac{r_{12.3} - (r_{14.3} \times r_{24.3})}{(1 - r_{14.3})(1 - r_{24.3}^2)}$$

Third, fourth, etc. order equations are also constructed by analogy. The calculative complexities raised by these equations are easily solved by modern computers.

We may then assume that we have data (for example) from a

survey on three variables, social class (V_1), ethnocentrism (V_2), and racial attitudes (V_3). If an argument were presented for the claim that higher social class position causes less ethnocentrism which, in turn, causes less prejudice, this could be represented as having the following path:

$$V_1 \rightarrow V_2 \rightarrow V_3$$

If we calculated correlations of $r_{12} = .78$, $r_{23} = .72$, and $r_{13} = .58$, we might claim that the path illustrated above already looks plausible. V_1 is highly correlated with V_2 (for the data collected) and V_2 highly correlated with V_3. Nevertheless, if there were no direct relation between V_1 and V_3 (if they were related only through V_2) we would expect the correlation between V_1 and V_3 to be lower, and our calculations seem to support this expectation. But the path illustrated is only one of several possible paths (which Blalock calls "models") which could be drawn between the three variables. An alternative path model might be

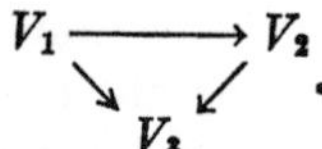

The only difference between the two path models is the added direct relation between V_1 and V_3. We might choose between the two by observing that the r_{13} correlation is lower than the other two, and therefore a direct relationship between V_1 and V_3 is less likely than the indirect relation in the first example. The partial correlation technique is supposed to make this inference more firm. If there is no relation between them, the correlation of V_1 and V_3 should be zero (or close to it) if V_2 is controlled. If we plug our correlation values into the equation we may calculate that

$$r_{13.2} = \frac{.58 - (.72 \times .78)}{(1 - .72^2)(1 - .78^2)} = .042.$$

Since $r_{13.2}$ is so close to zero, it is claimed that the first model ($V_1 \rightarrow V_2 \rightarrow V_3$) is more plausible. Blalock uses this technique but also introduces Herbert Simon's requirement that $r_{13} = (r_{12} \times r_{23})$.

(In this case $r_{13} = .58$ and the product of r_{12} and r_{23} is .56, so this condition is also closely met.) Simon's requirement is not, however, as it might seem, an independent condition. Using the partial correlation equation, it is clear that if $r_{13.2} = 0$, then the equation can be solved for r_{13} resulting in the statement that $r_{13} = (r_{12} \times r_{23})$. These two tests are, in fact, identical, and the empiricist who performs them both is clearly demonstrating his limited knowledge of the meaning of the equations he uses.

Blalock uses correlation and partial correlation as a basis for path analysis, and he subsequently infers that the paths thus derived were causally formed in the data. Most of Blalock's discoveries pertaining to causal inferences follow the same logic, although he also adds that attention should be paid to comparing regression coefficients which he feels are even more important than correlation for causal analysis.[2]

Blalock calls the results of his method causal *inference,* which is weaker than causal attribution. This relative weakness results in part from the observation that correlations (unlike causes) are not directional. The argument that social class causes ethnocentrism, which causes racial prejudice, is directional from class to prejudice, not because the statistical manipulations indicate a direction (correlation values are not vectors) but presumably because it is implausible that racial prejudice would cause ethnocentrism and consequently class position. Nevertheless, if this study had been done in South Africa or in some parts of the United States where qualification for social advancement and maintenance of social position depend on racist attitudes, the "causal" chain from racial prejudice to ethnocentrism to social class is just as plausible as the alternative. Even then, these two are not the only alternatives consistent with the correlational test which could just as easily be used to support such path models as

$$\begin{array}{ccc} & V_2 & \\ \swarrow & & \searrow \\ V_1 & & V_3 \end{array}$$

and

$$\begin{array}{ccc} V_1 & & V_3 \\ & \searrow \ \swarrow & \\ & V_2 & \end{array}$$

Statistically these are just as plausible as the first two because, although V_1 and V_3 are "highly related" to V_2, they are unrelated to one another when V_2 is controlled. In fact, the only argument against this alternative

[2] See Hubert M. Blalock, Jr., *Causal Inferences in Nonexperimental Research* (Chapel Hill, N.C.: University of North Carolina Press, 1961), p. 87.

is not statistical at all but stated in terms of common sense or some prejudicial notion held by the researcher.

Anyone seriously interested in explaining racism would be completely unable to do so by this method, which is unable to transcend correlations between particular bits of data to the level of explaining racism as a concept tied to other concepts rather than ephemeral observables. No causal model could ever explain racism as a necessary consequence of an exploitative stratification structure, and in that sense it is clearly a safe research technique for those tied in with such a structure.

Because the statistical method used is symmetric and does not result in a unique solution, Blalock calls it a method of causal *inference*. This means that instead of attributing a causal influence to a variable we claim that it *may be* a cause. In the above example the method may be used to reduce the twelve possible causal links to only four "probable" ones. The justification for using such an apparently indecisive technique must stand or fall on the usefulness of Blalock's special meaning of cause. It does not appear much more helpful to know that there are four probable causal chains (out of limited data—some important variables may not even have been considered) for a particular set of data than that there are twelves possible ones.

Blalock's discussion of cause precedes his presentation of his method and its conclusions are intended to be consistent with it. His causal discussion itself, however, is not internally consistent and involves a number of basic confusions. For example, having asserted that there is an "inherent gap" between theoretical and operational statements, he goes on to say that "causal thinking belongs completely on the theoretical level." [3] He then proceeds to the claim that "producing refers to an ontological process, i.e., to what exists in the real world" [4] and later incorporates the idea of "producing" in his definition of cause: "X is a direct cause of *Y* if and only if a change in *X* produces a change in the mean value of *Y*." [5] In other words, Blalock asserts that theoretical statements are inherently separated from empirical ones, causes are wholly theoretical, "pro-

[3] *Ibid.*, p. 6.
[4] *Ibid.*, p. 9.
[5] *Ibid.*, p. 19.

ducing" is empirical, and causes are causes because they produce effects. Clearly there is some confusion in this reasoning.

His discussion of the "causal principle" is equally confused. He refers to Philipp Frank's point that the principle of causality is not itself capable of proof but is assumed, instead, as a research tool. Blalock then ingeniously equates the causal principle with the problem of causal determination and argues with choice logic that if we cannot prove the causal principle then we cannot attribute causes in individual cases. Unfortunately, however, the causal principle is an assumption (not open to proof) that there are cause–effect relations between observables. The empiricist researcher makes this assumption before attempting to search for order in the world in terms of causes. Given such an assumption, what is needed is a method to unambiguously establish causes; otherwise the assumption is not justified. If we assume the world is made of cause–effect relations, yet our methods do not establish such relations, then either our method is useless for supporting the assumption or the assumption is useless for supporting the method. This is true for Blalock's method in relation to the assumption. Even worse, he gets himself into an incredible mess by assuming that his method is identical to the assumption which would have to lie behind it (but doesn't). Blalock may adhere to the causal principle, but his method neither legitimizes it nor follows from it.

Causes, according to Blalock, are not only both theoretical and empirical but in addition are always hypothetical. They can never be tested empirically because there could always be some other cause (either observed or unobserved) really doing the producing. Considering the taut reasoning found elsewhere in his work it would come as no surprise to find out that one reason he describes causal statements as theoretical is that they are not subject to empirical test in the above sense. Of course, the nontestability of causal relations is a consequence of the meaning he gives to "cause" rather than of the theoretical nature of causal statements. Nevertheless, granting the plausibility of the claim that causal statements cannot be empirically tested, what utility can be claimed for the relations to which causality has been inferred? Here Blalock becomes bogged down in a muddle of the problems of strength of relationship and scope. First he states that without experimental circumstances there are difficulties in evaluating a "causal law" stated in "universalistic terminology" [6] (a statement concerned with scope) and concludes as a consequence that causal laws should be stated "statistically" by which he means in terms of "probability" (a statement relevant to the strength of the relationship).[7]

Blalock states that a causal relation, direct in one model, may be indirect in another.[8] (In other words, the directness of a causal relation is arbitrary.) Then he defines causal relationships: "*X* is a direct cause of *Y* if and only if a change in *X* produces a change in the mean value of *Y*." [9] It does not require great intellectual effort to note that, if the directness of a causal relation is arbitrary, the term "direct" in his definition has no meaning. We might note in addition that the meaning of *X* and *Y* is rather confused: if *Y* has a mean value, it must represent a set, but does *X* represent a set, the mean value of a set, or simply an individual case? How, then, can we even begin to use this definition?

But the problems of Blalock's conception of cause go beyond the confusions and contradictions of his exposition. The problem of the meaning of cause (and producing) in survey research and the problem of scope are still unsolved in spite of (or because of) his exposition. He asserts that the "forcing or producing idea is not contained in the notion of temporal sequence" and that his idea of cause will "not depend on temporal sequences." [10] But, although forcing or producing may not be entailed in temporal sequences, temporal sequence is clearly entailed in the ideas of forcing and producing (and consequently in Blalock's notion of cause). David Hume, John Stuart Mill, and most other philosophers (and most people, in fact) understand that forcing and producing are processes and that processes (by definition) take place over time. Blalock was concerned mainly with cross-sectional studies (which have no time dimension) and apparently thought that because his empirical data were not gathered over time, the time dimension could be removed from the meaning of cause. The meaning of

[6] *Ibid.*, pp. 17–18.

[7] *Ibid.*, p. 18.

[8] *Ibid.*, p. 19.

[9] *Ibid.*

[10] *Ibid.*, p. 10.

cause, however, should not follow from his empirical method but should determine it. It is certainly illegitimate for a good empiricist to fudge around the meaning of cause because his research techniques do not measure up to the previously accepted meaning. Blalock's meaning of cause is not the same as that used anywhere else. Either he is speaking of a "cause" or he should use a new term for his idea. A sow's ear remains a sow's ear, even if sold as a silk purse.

Hume and Mill clearly intended causal relations to have unlimited scope, but the empirical methods devised by the statisticians did not produce such results, and the idea of cause was dropped while considerably less emphasis was placed on induction as a definitive process. Blalock has attempted to resurrect the idea of cause from its well-earned grave. Unfortunately the idea has merely decayed in the intervening years and smells no sweeter than it did thirty years ago. Blalock's "causal inferences" are no more than descriptive statements about the frequency distributions of a unique sample from a unique population. If this is all that can be patched together from the old idea of cause, it would have been better if he had let it rest in peace.[11]

[11] Apart from the problems concerned with his use of cause, Blalock's technique faces the same problems as the other techniques outlined in Chapter 5, and, in fact, it must be concluded that his technique is no more capable of establishing association between empirical categories than the elaboration technique. The method of "causal inference" cannot result in empirical generalization.

probability in empiricism and science[1]

6 The relational and associational procedures of systematic empiricism are statistical procedures justified by the belief that observable events may be viewed as more or less probable and that a value can be attached to that probability. It is usually assumed that the uses of statistical procedures in social science are logically sound because the physical sciences use probability theory. Not only is this assumption based on a misinterpretation of the use of probability in physics, but the use of probability in systematic empiricism is logically and mathematically unsound. The claim that the method is systematic (and thus objective) because of its use of statistics is therefore justified only by ignorance.

Probability in Empiricism

The notion of probability in sociology is consistent with the empiricist belief that scientific knowledge is gained by inference from the direct observation of individual facts. This leads to a

[1] This chapter was written by Dr. Cesar Hernandez-Cela, Assistant Professor, University of Kansas.

conception of induction by the enumeration of observations until a level of confidence is reached. It is a generalizing procedure in which n instances of phenomenon A are observed with phenomenon B, a point at which the observer feels that he can claim that "all *A*s are associated with *B*s." It is believed that such generalizations can be accepted as "probable" depending on the number of instances observed. By asserting that a generalization is true at a certain "probability" the empiricist is able to assign a value to it by which he qualifies his ignorance. He may observe a population, n, of churchgoing individuals, of which n_1 of them give alms to the poor, in order to establish a relationship between A (going to church) and B (giving alms) based on the proportion, $\frac{n_1}{n}$, of observed churchgoers who gave alms to the poor. The proportion, however, is not relevant to churchgoers or almsgivers not in the sample. The value n_1 is not equivalent to B, and n is not equivalent to A. He therefore assigns the probability, $\frac{n_1}{n}$, to the population he studied and assumes that it is only hypothetical for the total possible population of *A*s and *B*s.

Since the universe of *A*s and *B*s is potentially infinite, n must approach infinity (or the total of all possible *A*s) for the ratio $\frac{n_1}{n}$ to hold for all *A*s. The relative frequency of n_1 to n $\left(\frac{n_1}{n}\right)$ is the probability of an event only if calculated cumulatively from an infinite number of observed events. In other words, *a relative frequency is a probability only if the number of events taken into account is infinite.* But when the number of instances is finite (as in the case of a population of churchgoers and almsgivers), the ratio is a relative frequency but not a probability. This definition of probability excludes all empirically obtained relative frequencies because it is impossible to obtain the infinite number, n, of observations which would be necessary to make a probability statement about the universe of *A*s. A relative frequency is a description, but a probability is a calculation. Although we may calculate a theoretical probability value of $\frac{1}{2}$ for a universe in which A and B are equally represented when the number of instances approaches infinity, the most that can be said about the number of heads that will turn up when tossing a coin twenty times is that there will be a particular frequency which is unknown until we toss the coin. In other words, the assignment of a value of $\frac{1}{2}$ simply because the coin has two sides is an error because we do not know that each side will be equally represented in any empirical case. Equal representation in probability is a mathematical assumption which is violated in finite empirical cases.

Pierre Laplace interpreted "probability" as the ratio of the number of favorable cases to the total number of cases, provided the cases are all equally likely. If we knew that the six faces of a die were equally likely, then we would know that the probability of a single face (the favorable outcome) is $\frac{1}{6}$. But equal likelihood, like equal probability, can only be specified theoretically since we can never determine equal likelihood through observation. We may instead find that tossing a die results in a successive run of fives and that it thus does not appear one-sixth of the time, and does not seem to be empirically equally likely.

Neither the relative frequency interpretation of the meaning of probability nor Laplace's provides a satisfactory basis for the empirical use of probability. These interpretations refer only to theoretical populations, and the use of the axioms of probability is therefore restricted to nonempirical populations. These axioms are:

1. The probability of an event A is a positive real number.
2. The probability of a *certain* event is one.
3. If A and B are mutually exclusive, then the joint probability of A and B equals the sum of the probabilities of each.

The theory of probability is built on these axioms just as Euclidean geometry is built on its axioms. This theory can be used in scientific theories, but it cannot be used to associate observables. Sociological statistical procedures are concerned with observables and therefore violate the conditions under which probability calculations may be legitimately used. But they are so often used that they are frequently accepted (in spite of their obvious absurdity) without question. We are told that the probability of rain tomorrow is 60 percent when, in fact, it will either rain or it will not. Such statements are unjustified, wrong, and misleading.

Social empiricists, when presenting numerical values such as the "probability" of churchgoers giving alms to the poor, might state that only in 5 percent of cases would an association as large as 60 percent or larger not obtain when instances are randomly selected. But, observing individuals, we may only say that they either do or do not give alms. In the first observation we may find that 60 percent of the total sample gave alms, but in succeeding observations this value may differ. We cannot, in fact, have any expectations of probability of giving alms to the poor, no matter how many samples we take. If, on the other hand, the sample approaches or is equal to the total population of churchgoers, then the figure represents a simple proportion, a frequency, not a probability. On the other hand, specification that only 5 percent of samples will not result in the .60 or more is meaningless. If we chose several samples all of the same size, and found that in only 5 percent of them the figure was under .60, then we still can draw no conclusions, for we know nothing about the empirical conditions prevailing in future samples. Such a claim has no basis either in theory or in observation. What the claim means is that if there were an infinite number of cases whose composition was on the average like that of the sample, then in only 5 percent of them would the percentage be smaller than .60. But, we cannot assume that any other empirical cases are on the average like the sample studied, and we cannot assume that they are infinite in number. Theoretical cases can be infinite in number, but empirical ones cannot. Such statistical claims, of course, cannot be violated empirically because they are not probability statements at all but disguised frequencies obtained by observation. Future observations cannot verify or falsify frequencies but only slightly modify their numerical value in the light of new cases. Furthermore, the statistical procedures themselves are not open to any kind of empirical verification or falsification and consequently can be safely supported by appeal to authority—at least we cannot empirically prove the authorities wrong.

Rudolf Carnap described such probability statements based on the relative frequency interpretation as "statistical probability" and "meaningless." On the other hand, he believed that "an elementary statement of statistical probability is factual and empirical; it says something about the facts of nature and hence must be based upon empirical procedure."[2] Carnap, believing the facts themselves to be of great importance, resolved his mental dilemma by proposing that one should instead speak of "inductive probability," *based* on the facts but resulting in a nonfactual probability statement for a hypothesis *h* on the basis of evidence *e*. This probability is, then, a completely "logical" idea. Thus he elevated probability to a status which was not dependent on the truth or falsity of facts. According to Carnap, "An elementary statement of inductive probability, e.g., one which attributes to two given arguments (*e* and *h*) a particular number (*i*) as a value of inductive probability is either logically true or logically false. . . . It is independent of the contingency of facts because it does not say anything about facts, although the two arguments (*e* and *h*) do, in general, refer to facts."[3] In other words, Carnap has claimed that, although inductive probability refers to facts, it says nothing about facts. This, indeed, is an accurate description of empiricist probability in general, regardless of tags.[4]

The role of probability in empirical induction diverts attention

[2] Rudolf Carnap, *Logical Foundations of Probabilty* (Chicago: University of Chicago Press, 1950), p. 32. The claim has been advanced that the problem of obtaining relative frequencies for a potentially infinite universe is solved by basing those frequencies on random samples; but random samples are nevertheless samples from finite populations, and, since infinite universes are theoretical rather than empirical, it is impossible to take random samples from them. For an excellent argument destroying Hans Reichenbach's and Leopold Von Mises' claims about the utility of probability in gaining knowledge about observed phenomena, see Bertrand Russell, *Human Knowledge* (New York: Simon and Schuster, 1948), pp. 412–18. Russell argues from the empiricist point of view that such "probability" statements (frequency statements) cannot ever give true empirical knowledge since each new observed case is added to the "known" probability statement, and thus the statement is never "true" but varies according to a possible infinite regress of cases.

[3] Carnap, *Logical Foundations of Probability,* p. 32.

[4] The property of probability statements of not allowing falsification or verification has been noticed by philosophers of science such as Karl Popper, *The Logic of Scientific Discovery* (New York: Harper & Row, Publishers, 1959), pp. 65–191; Richard B. Braithwaite, *Scientific Explanation* (New York: Harper & Row, Publishers, 1960), p. 151; Carl G. Hempel, *Aspects of Scientific Explanation* (New York: The Free Press, 1965), ch. 2; and others. The empiricist leanings of these authors have prevented them from realizing that the problem of indecisiveness inherent in probability statements is but a sanctified escape from the problem of induction. The logical empiricists Carnap, Keynes, and Jeffreys have recognized the problem involved in probability statements about observable facts.

from the scientific inadequacy of empiricism. Probability is simply used as a justification for action in the face of the unknown, for empiricist knowledge does not extend beyond that which has been observed. This is absolute indeterminism at the observational level. But empiricism has gained a great deal by the introduction of probability. Whereas inductions to universal generalizations are always in danger of falsification because only a single instance is sufficient to deny them, "probabilistic" generalizations are only "probably" true and therefore can never be verified or falsified by observation, although they may be found to be "probably" false.

Stephen Toulmin explains:

> . . . little is altered by the introduction of mathematics into the discussion of the probability of future events. The numerical discussion of probabilities becomes, no doubt, sophisticated and somewhat complex, but unless a calculus provides a means of estimating how far propositions are entitled to our trust or belief, it can hardly be called a "calculus of probabilities" at all. The development of the mathematical theory of probability accordingly leaves the force of our probability-statements unchanged; its value is that it greatly refines the standards to be appealed to, and so the morals we can draw about the degree of expectability of future events.[5]

If we may agree that the introduction of the idea of mathematical probability to what is actually no more than an educated empiricist guess adds nothing to it but a false security, then R. A. Fisher's supposed solution to the problem of association is, in fact, no more than an ideological justification for ignoring the logic of mathematical probability. Far from attempting to empirically interpret probability, Fisher in his "fiducial" argument claimed that probability can be constructed out of available data. Thus Fisher rejected the notion that there is any difference between a proportion and a probability.

Probability in Science

Because the empiricist conceives of scientific theories as constructed inductively from observed relationships between facts, he

[5] Stephen Toulmin, *The Uses of Argument* (Cambridge: Cambridge University Press, 1969), p. 91.

interprets the theoretical concepts of other sciences as observables. Consequently, when the empiricist hears that the developed sciences (physics and chemistry) also use probability, he concludes that they (physicists) have recognized that statements about facts are always probable, never certain. Their hypotheses, like ours, it is assumed, are probable, although the probability is higher because of the more objective facts with which they deal. Claims are also made that in the developed sciences, just as in sociology, laws are induced by statistical inference, and that these laws are nothing but regularities with differing degrees of probability.

According to Hubert Blalock, for example:

> . . . a far more important function of statistics . . . is that of induction of inferring properties of a population on the basis of known sample results [sic]. . . . Inductive statistics is based directly on probability theory. We thus have a purely deductive discipline providing a rational basis for induction. To the writer's knowledge there is no other rational basis for induction . . . why is it that sciences such as physics and chemistry have been able to get along so well without the extensive use of statistical techniques? . . . But this seems to be primarily a matter of good fortune [!] . . . It should be emphasized, however, that many of the same statistical principles apply to laboratory experiments in physics. . . . For example, if an experiment in physics has been replicated thirty-seven times with similar results, it is nevertheless conceivable that subsequent trials will yield different outcomes. The scientist must therefore generalize on the basis of a limited number of experiments, and the inferences he makes are essentially statistical in nature [sic]. . . . Basically, then, statistical inference underlies all scientific generalizations [sic].[6]

If the physicist were to follow Blalock's prescription to learn something about the motion of physical bodies, he would first observe a sample of bodies in motion and record facts about those bodies, such as color, weight, size, shape, the distance each body has moved, the direction of movement, the time elapsed, their heat, and other innumerable observable characteristics, and then he would test for all of the possible statistical associations between the facts

[6] Hubert M. Blalock, Jr., *Social Statistics* (New York: McGraw-Mill Book Co., 1960), pp. 5–6.

he recorded. He would discover either that no significant associations were found, or that some associations were significant at a certain level of probability p.

Subsequently the empiricist-physicist may decide to replicate his study thirty-seven times with thirty-seven samples of bodies falling. Once this is done, he may examine the association between the variables' weight and time of fall after having controlled several other variables. Even if a negative association between weight and time of fall appeared in every replication (although the level of association observed in one particular sample may differ from that observed in another, it remained negative), it is nevertheless possible that subsequent trials will yield different outcomes. He will therefore calculate a "probability," p, the probability of a heavy body falling faster than a light body. He therefore can never make a determinative statement about whether weight is related to time of fall but only that it might be.

Probability in physics, however, is not the empiricist probability of social science. According to Albert Einstein,

> Altogether I really do not at all like the now fashionable [modische] "positivistic" tendency of clinging to what is observable. I regard it as trivial that one cannot, in the range of atomic magnitudes, make predictions with any desired degree of precision, and I think . . . that theory cannot be fabricated out of the results of observation, but that it can only be invented.[7]

Such statements are often hastily interpreted by empiricists who conclude that in physics, too, accurate prediction of observable phenomena is not possible and conclude that statistical inference underlies all scientific generalizations. But Einstein's statement explicitly denies such conclusions in denying the use of observation as the basis of theory.

Probability in statistical and quantum mechanics does not apply to observable phenomena but to theoretical constructs (concepts) which are neither based on observation nor definable in terms of

[7] A letter to Popper reproduced in Karl Popper, *The Logic of Scientific Discovery*, p. 458.

observable phenomena.[8] Probability is used simply as a theoretical calculative device while its theoretical derivations are related abstractively to observable phenomena. The question as to the probability of empirical phenomena never arises. Isomorphism is established between a determinative theory and the phenomena to be explained.

Failure to predict certain phenomena may arise from limits on our powers of observation, but in this respect quantum physics and Newtonian mechanics are equally indeterministic.[9] Many of the philosophical debates about quantum mechanics are concerned with the elucidation of problems at the theoretical level. Particles, quantum states, probability, and other theoretical concepts are discussed with the aid of analogies derived from macroscopic phenomena, for example, elastic balls, motion, collision, measurement interference, experiment, and so on.[10] But the use of analogies derived from

[8] An empiricistic attempt to arrive at a formulation of quantum mechanics in which only observable quantities (in the macroscopic sense) enter the theoretical description was initiated, surprisingly enough, by Werner Heisenberg, one of the founders of the theory. "It is interesting, however, that . . . Heisenberg's original goal to replace the conventional (theoretical) structure of quantum mechanics has not been reached." John L. Powell and Bern Crasenam, *Quantum Mechanics* (Reading, Mass.: Addison-Wesley Publishing Co., 1961). It was against Heisenberg's empiricistic attempt that Einstein directed his 1935 letter to Karl Popper.

[9] For a good clarification of the misinterpretations that have led to the attribution of determinism to classical mechanics and of indeterminism to quantum mechanics, see Ernest Nagel, *The Structure of Science* (New York: Harcourt Brace Jovanovich, 1961), pp. 277–335. Essentially, determinism or indeterminism refers to the theoretical assumptions of the scientific theory. It should not refer to the observable phenomena which the theory can explain or predict. Whether a theory is deterministic or indeterministic, in the above sense, does not have any bearing on its ability to establish isomorphism with observable phenomena. If the observable initial conditions are known, a theory is uniquely isomorphic to facts (since it is a theory); otherwise, it is not. For example, if we do not know, or cannot determine, the initial conditions required to determine how a leaf would fall, we could not determine its exact way of falling, even if the theory of gravitation that could do so is said to be deterministic. The same situation applies to modern physics. Democritus's atoms moved in a straight line; thus, his physical theory could be called determinist. Epicurus's atoms were postulated to move freely without specific determination; thus, his physical theory could be called indeterministic.

[10] By analogies we simply mean illustrations by means of macroscopic entities, not to be confused with models that behave according to classical laws. Modern physics arose precisely when certain phenomena suggested by the available theories could not be explained by any classical model.

macroscopic observables does not lead the physicist to confuse theory with probabilistic generalization.[11] The empiricist misinterpretation of science is a result of the inability of the empiricist to think in terms other than observables. If probability is properly understood as a theoretical conception, it is no more a reflection of observable experience than any other theoretical construct used in science. Since it is part of a theoretical calculus it does not have to be based on facts; it is not intended to be so.[12]

[11] Classically, the state of a system at a particular instant is known if the position and the velocity of each of its component parts are given at that instant. In quantum theory a state is illustrated by the use of the classical analogy with the postulation that the position and velocity are not known. But even so, position and velocity do not have the same meaning as in classical mechanics; the words are maintained for the convenience of illustration.

[12] This language has also misled philosophers of science of the logical positivistic or logical empiricistic school. But "no philosopher has yet succeeded in giving a satisfactory 'logical reduction' of theoretical concepts to 'hard experiential data' alone. On the contrary, there is increasingly strong reason to think that this cannot be done. Our theoretical concepts always turn out in practice to have been framed *in advance* of the experiences that justify them; indeed, it has been indispensable that they should be framed in advance if we are to pose any theoretical relevant questions about those experiences." Stephen Toulmin, ed., *Physical Reality: Philosophical Essays on Twentieth-Century Physics* (New York: Harper & Row, Publishers, 1970), p. xi.

the search for measurement through scaling

7 The meaning of measurement in sociology has its origin in the writings and ideas of the "operationalists" and results in various scaling procedures. *Operationalism* is concerned in general with the formation of empirical categories through experience and in particular with determining systematic operations to be carried out in order to achieve those empirical categories. The basic assumption behind these procedures is that empirical categories can best be defined by the operations used to observe the experiences to be included in the categories. The purpose of operational procedures is to structure these operations so that different results can be assigned numerical values. When a succession of similar operations can be performed on a succession of similar objects with each different result being assigned a different numerical value, the aggregate of all of those possible values is called a "scale." The "scale," in turn, is supposed to represent a "concept." Thus, "the concept IQ is what the IQ test measures" or "status is what the North–Hatt scale measures." Like the empiricists, the operationalists have confused concepts with observationals. If IQ is defined by an empirical thing, the operations of the IQ

test, then it too is an observational. As such, it cannot enter into mathematical relations with other concepts in a scientific law. In fact, operationalists, like empiricists, view scientific laws as consisting of causal empirical relations between observables. It is an approach to measurement which is based on the supposition that theories and measures (and indeed all of science) are empirical discoveries—regularities uncovered in nature.

The "operations" proposed by the operationalists are simply rules by means of which empiricists can make observations. Operationalism, then, is merely a branch of empiricism which concentrates on the measurement of observational categories.

The early operationalist Norman Campbell defines a scientific law as "a proposition asserting a relation of uniform association which can be established by experiment." [1] The terms of laws are "complex collections" of judgments of sensations: "The discovery of laws is a special case of induction [sic] or the determination of a general relation from a limited number of particulars." [2] It is clear that Campbell is also an empiricist and furthermore that he agrees fundamentally with John Stuart Mill. He differs from Mill mainly in that he rejects the notion of cause in favor of "uniform association." He limited his discussion to an established area of science, physics, and thus missed Pearson's insight that all empirical relations are necessarily those of "correlation or contingency."

Percy Bridgman further popularized operationalism in the 1920s and 1930s, claiming that "experience is determined only by experience." [3] He believed that the first lesson of relativity is that experiment into new domains results in new facts.[4] Or, according to Bridgman, Einstein "found precisely how the operations for judging simultaneity change when the observer moves." [5] Of course, Einstein, who was not an experimentalist, *found* nothing about simultaneity; instead, his theory of relativity (fitting his own definition of theory) was *invented.*

[1] Norman Robert Campbell, *Foundations of Science* (New York: Dover Publications, 1957), p. 38.

[2] *Ibid.*, p. 88.

[3] Percy W. Bridgman, *The Logic of Modern Physics* (New York: The Macmillan Company, 1927), p. 3.

[4] *Ibid.*, p. 2.

[5] *Ibid.*, p. 8.

Herbert Dingle, a more modern operationalist, believed that laws are relations found between the elements of experience, and that these relations are found by idealizing our experience in order to simplify it. Accordingly, Galileo did not study leaves falling in the wind "but instead made grooves in smooth inclined planes and rolled spherical balls along them."[6] The use of mathematics in science is to help find empirical relations through experiment. All three of these prominent operationalists held empiricist conceptions of science. Thus they had to view concepts as observables. The assertion that concepts had to be defined operationally was thus consistent with their empiricism. Since physics (also chemistry and biology) already had established theories and measurements, their empiricism did little harm in their own fields, but it is not surprising that Campbell and Bridgman contributed nothing of theoretical value to their field.

Although the operationalist view of scientific measurement did little more than possibly inhibit the development of theories in established fields (and then only in the countries where it was most popular and taught in the universities, England and the United States), it had a disastrous impact on less developed fields such as psychology and the social sciences. In these fields operationalism has been consistently (and persistently) used as a *method,* whereas in other fields operationalists have only interpreted already established measurement procedures. Operationalism has been used as a justification for the development of "scaling" techniques in the social sciences, and it is precisely in these areas that there is a "measurement problem."

The addition of operationalism to modern systematic empiricism resulted in an internally consistent system readily usable for attempts to generate new knowledge through observation. It was enthusiastically adopted in psychology and sociology. No empiricist method for generating measures was available until operationalism came along. Because systematic empiricism uses "empirical probability" as the basis for association and averaging techniques for assessing relatedness, the psychologists and sociologists who wished to use it needed to obtain from their observations either numbers

[6] Herbert Dingle, "A Theory of Measurement," *British Journal for the Philosophy of Science,* vol. 1, no. 1 (May 1950), p. 12.

or something which could pass for numbers. Before beginning empiricist statistical procedures, it is necessary to have a *scale* to administer. Since the operationalist thinks a scale is a means of measurement and, as Dingle put it, "*measurement is any precisely specified operation that yields a number,*"[7] it follows that the early operationalists had only to precisely specify an operation and claim that it resulted in a number, and the data-gathering process could begin. The gathered data, responses to categories (which because they were "scaled" were treated more or less as numbers), in turn entered into the statistical procedures of empirical generalization.

Measurement procedures in science result in numbers which enter into equations for calculative purposes. Scaling procedures in empiricist fields such as sociology and psychology do not result in numbers but, at best, in ranked categories. These categories are assigned numerals (through various techniques), and the result is called an "ordinal" or an "interval" scale. The numerals from these scales, however, are not used in equations for mathematical calculation (which indeed would be illegitimate) but are used according to the standardized procedures of statistical empiricism.

The criterion that a term is what its measurement procedures make it, is not a clear guide to the methods of scale construction. In fact, in spite of the bellicose defenses of its advocates, operationalism has not been worked out as a systematic approach. (Perhaps this is an advantage in empiricism—at least it closes no doors.) It is nevertheless clear that the typical scale-seeking operationalist begins with two guides to his behavior: (1) to establish a scale *about something* (or a property of something), and (2) to have as a result something that at least looks like numbers so that he can apply the tools of systematic empiricism to get at his finding about the world.

Scaling Techniques

We might, for example, wish to construct a scale for measuring the status (a property) of occupations (our "something"). We may begin by constructing a "summated rating scale" for which we

[7] *Ibid.*, p. 11.

choose one hundred occupations and ask a random sample of American citizens to rank them according to their status. After collecting our data we may obtain a composite rank by assigning the value of 1 to the occupation (or category) having the smallest summed value and 100 to the category having the largest. We may then use this "scale" to evaluate the status of a respondent who will be given a "score" representing his occupation, which can then be related to other such "scores" through certain statistical procedures in our search for an empirical association.

A more complex scale could be constructed using the Guttman technique. In this example we are hoping to end up with a scale for "social distance" after asking a random sample of Americans the following questions:

1. Would you object to having black people in your state?
2. Would you object to having black people in your town?
3. Would you object to having black people work where you work?
4. Would you object to having black people in your neighborhood?
5. Would you object if your daughter married a black man?

These questions are supposed to tap the "dimension" of prejudice or social distance and only that "dimension." It is expected that more people will answer more favorably to the first questions than to the last ones, and, if they "scale" in that sense, the scale is thought to have the quality of "unidimensionality." In a perfect Guttman scale, items are ranked from stronger to weaker (or from more to less, and so on) in such a way that any respondent's response pattern is "reproducible" from knowledge of only his most extreme response. For example, the respondent who was willing to work with a black is not supposed to object to having blacks living in his town or state. The respondent not objecting to 5 is not supposed to object to items 1, 2, 3, or 4. A perfect scale establishes a clear order and is claimed to possess the quality of transitivity (see below) which the occupational scale does not. In practice, of course, there are no perfect Guttman scales, for any consistent empirical response pattern is capable of being reversed by the next respondent or the same respondent's next answer (for example, in the case of a man who hates both blacks and his daughter). These are called "errors," and various indexes have been devised to indicate the quality of the scale (according to the proportion of errors) by means of more or less complicated averaging techniques.

A third type of scaling technique is called the "paired comparison" method. That technique begins with a set of statements about some things which are presented, two at a time, to a sample of respondents until all possible pairs are exhausted. The respondents are asked to judge which statement of each pair is "more favorable" or has more of the property to be scaled. For example, of the two statements, "I suppose China should be allowed in the UN" and "The Chinese are tricky, dangerous people," presumably the first would usually be judged as more favorable toward the attitude object, the Chinese. After a great number of people have judged a pair of statements (i, j), some might say that one (i) was more favorable while others choose the other one (j). If f_{ij} is the frequency with which i is chosen and N is the number of respondents then P_{ij}, the proportion judging i to be more favorable, equals $\frac{f_{ij}}{N}$. The crucial idea of the method of paired comparisons is that P_{ij} can be represented as the standard score, Z_{ij}. Given this (plus a group of assumptions), it is concluded that $Z_{ij} = \overline{S}_i - \overline{S}_j$. In other words, the proportion, P_{ij}, has been expressed as a Z score which now is represented as the distance between $\overline{S}_i$ and $\overline{S}_j$ which are supposed to be points on a continuum or the scale values of the two attitude objects. S_i and S_j are called the "modal discriminal processes" for each statement. If we have four statements, then there will be six equations of the form, $Z_{ij} = \overline{S}_j - \overline{S}_{ij}$, and we consequently may solve for the values of the S terms. After introducing a constant to shift the zero point around, we then tell ourselves that we have a "scale." If this reasoning seems rather fuzzy, we may point out that the idea behind the procedure is that the "closer" items are to one another, the more often the respondents will mix them up and present us with a value for P_{ij} which approaches .5. As P_{ij} approaches .5, Z approaches zero and the separation of the $\overline{S}$s $(\overline{S}_i - \overline{S}_j)$ approaches zero, meaning that the items come closer and closer to the same position. On the other hand, as the respondents come into closer agreement, P_{ij} approaches 1 (or zero) and Z gets rapidly larger. (A. L. Edwards' book, *Techniques of Attitude Scale Construction,* the standard text, advises us to ignore Ps larger than .98 because at that point small changes in the value of P bring very large changes in Z.) The logic of paired comparisons is not too complicated; its basis is the notion that position on a scale can be estimated from the empirical "errors" made by respondents to questionnaires.

The scale, once constructed, is considered to have the qualities of an "interval" scale. Its application consists of no more than ranking respondents according to the item or items they choose from the set of items as they were ranked when originally applied to other individuals.

From an empiricist–operationalist point of view, a scale should be judged according to three criteria: dimensionality, stability, and order. Since the operationalist assumes that a term's meaning is equivalent to a set of operations, then if he is to uncover one term instead of several, there must be some basis in the operation (or scaling procedure) for claiming that only one property is measured. If the scale is to be useful, it should retain its particular scale qualities under varying conditions of application not limited to particular times and places. On the other hand, if it is to enter into statistical relations, it must have at least the minimum requirements of a scale, an order. Using S. S. Stevens' terms, an "ordinal" scale is one in which precedence is established for the included categories and in which the precedence is transitive, that is, if $A < B$ and $B < C$, then $A < C$ must hold. In an "interval" scale the categories or points on the scale are such that they can be added. A scale with "ratio" qualities is one which has all the qualities of a rational number system. These types of scales are viewed as being in an ascending order of complexity and exactness, each higher type having all the (good) qualities of the lower one. Thus, this view of scaling itself has the qualities of an ordinal scale going from (1) an ordinal scale having precedence and transitivity, to (2) an interval scale having precedence, transitivity, and interval, to (3) the final state of perfection, a ratio scale having precedence, transitivity, intervals, a "natural" zero point, and so on.

These three criteria (dimensionality, stability, and order) are consistent with the empiricist–operationalist system within which the three examples of types of scales were devised. The utility of such scales is dependent on how well these criteria are met. If the scale is of a single property or dimension, then its term will have a clear operational meaning. If it orders effectively, objects can be compared and their properties related. If it is stable, the quantities measured can be compared with quantities measured at other times and places with the same scale. A simple yardstick easily meets all these criteria and attains a "ratio" level as a scale. Evidence of these qualities should be found in the techniques of scale construction because, to the operationalist, the meaning comes from the operations themselves.

According to these criteria, then, the method of summated ratings is a failure. The only method of determining dimensionality in the construction of the status scale was the request that the respondents rank the occupations according to "status." It is clear that the meaning of status to the respondents could vary widely, and that the only dimensionality which could be involved is in the mind of the researcher. In fact, the problem of intersubjectivity is present in all response-based scaling.

Order in a summated rating scale is also based on the feelings of the respondents about the way status should be ranked. Even if this were an adequate basis for a scale, there is no operation to establish or test transitivity, so it must be concluded that even an ordinal level of scaling has not been reached. This type of scale also fails to meet the stability criterion. A "scale" similar to the "status scale" was, for example, presented to a group of "middle-class whites" and a group of "hippies" with the not altogether surprising discovery that their response patterns were completely different (and empirically unrelated). Since both groups were midwestern Americans, there is no reason to expect the scale to hold in other societies. In summary, the summated rating scale has none of the properties required of a useful empirical scaling method.

From the point of view of science, the summated rating scale is no more than the result of a routinized averaging procedure. One does not measure length by asking a sample of people to rank basketball players, Supreme Court justices, children, midgets, rabbits, turtles, ants, and so on according to their beliefs about which has the greatest length and then summing the result to get a "scale" of the way the average person in the sample thought they should be ranked. No amount of refining could make this procedure even fractionally as useful as a yardstick. The idea that one could eventually get a ranking of length with units and mathematical properties by collecting more and more data such as this is clearly preposterous. Applying this method to determine a "scale" to "measure status" is equally preposterous.

Proponents of the Guttman scaling technique claim that it results in a unidimensional scale. What this means is that a set of items which scale at a high level of reproducibility are claimed to represent a single property or dimension. Although this claim is often accepted today, Guttman himself was more careful and argued that inspection of the content of the scaled items is crucial. Actually, this inspection of the item content (itself highly subjective and therefore uncertain) is the only basis for determining dimensionality. Guttman's followers seem to think that they can claim that the technique results in unidimensionality whenever it results in a rank ordering of items. In actuality the claim of unidimensionality is merely a tag put on the "scale" when the results are ordered. Although it is true, as Guttman claimed, that items which scale together will not necessarily correlate, the converse statement that items which correlate will not scale does not follow and is not true. Thus two different sets of items which correlate highly will scale together, and therefore scales differing widely in content (or dimensionality) will scale together if they correlate.[8] Consequently the claim of unidimensionality simply does not hold up, even though some operationalists take the mindless position that things that correlate highly are necessarily the same. There is no guarantee in the operations of Guttman scaling that a scale will have a single dimension or even that it will have any known or identifiable number of dimensions.

A scale with perfect reproducibility is characterized by precedence and transitivity and is an "ordinal scale." Scales without perfect reproducibility are not even "ordinal scales." Repeated studies have shown that a set of items which scales for one population will not necessarily scale for another and, in fact, usually will

[8] See Ray G. Francis and Robert C. Stone, "Measurement and Attitude Analysis," *Midwest Sociologist,* vol. 18, no. 1 (1956), pp. 16–26.

not. Even then, following David Hume's argument, it is clear that for any empirical technique of data gathering, results (such as perfect reproducibility) which we find at one time may not be found at another. This means that, although a Guttman scale can be constructed from the responses given by a population to a set of items, the "scale" cannot be used subsequently to measure the position of one or more members of any new population. Each new application of the "scale" is instead simply a test of it in which the previous order may be falsified. But this is clearly a caricature of measurement. The idea of testing a yardstick against each new situation to see if it will still "scale" is ludicrous. Guttman scaling is, in fact, not a measuring technique at all, but a technique for summarizing data by combining the responses of a population to a set of objects in such a way that, on the average and ignoring errors, an ordinal ranking is achieved. But post-factum ranking is not measurement.

The test for dimensionality of the paired comparison technique is concerned with circular triads. A circular triad occurs in a response pattern when the respondent judges an item *A* less favorably than another item *B*, *B* less than *C*, but *C* less than *A* ($A < B$, $B < C$, $C < A$). According to a rule of thumb, a certain proportion of such triads indicates that the scale must contain more than one dimension (the proportion having been arbitrarily established by authority). If fewer triads are present, then it is assumed that only one dimension is present. The rationale is that the order of the first two pairs is explained by a response to one dimension while the apparent reversal in the third paired comparison is explained by response to another dimension. Even if one were to accept such reasoning, it is nevertheless obvious that if a scale contained two highly positively correlated dimensions it would not result in circular triads. The paired comparison technique fails as miserably as the Guttman technique to meet the criterion of dimensionality. The presence of a single dimension can only be claimed to be a result of the subjective judgment involved in determining its content.

Order in the paired comparison method is determined only subjectively by the preferential judgments of the respondents (and this has no meaning for a new population) while transitivity can be checked by the presence of circular triads. But this technique is claimed to be able to be used to "reach" the "interval level" in which distance between the response categories is calculated from disagreements between the respondents concerning the order of those categories. Order is established through the agreement of respondents' preferences, while interval distance is established because of the disagreement of their preferences. In other words, we calculate how far apart two items are because of the amount of disagreement about which precedes (or is larger or stronger than) the other.

But since order is not unambiguously established, this technique does not satisfy the criterion of an ordinal scale, much less an interval one! What order there is, is particular to a unique population and there is no reason to expect that order to be stable between populations. The paired comparisons technique is no more than a post-factum procedure for summarizing data—it is not a measuring technique at all.

There are, of course, other scaling techniques used in both sociology and psychology, but they also fail to result in measurement. If a scale is to be used for measurement it must not only have the mathematical properties of a scale but it must be capable of measuring one population after another—that is, it must not be dependent on or altered by any population; however, this is impossible to achieve by any empirical scaling technique. Scaling techniques are *all* dependent on particular populations for the scales they produce. They are not techniques for achieving measurement but are simply ways of averaging and compositing which result, at most, in an overall descriptive approximate ranking for particular populations.

Empiricists ordinarily discuss scaling from the point of view of "validity" and "reliability." The validity issue usually boils down to questions such as, "How can we know that our status measure really measures status?" This question is meaningless, even to the operationalist, for it is evident that from his point of view status can be no more than its operations of measurement. Obviously it must measure status because "status is what it measures." "Reliability" is considered even more crucial, and questions here usually are concerned with whether the same group will score similarly at two different times and sometimes with the issues of ordering and stability. The primary question is meaningless in any case, because no empirical group is ever the same at two different times. But, even within the limits of most discussions, it is clear that existing scaling procedures are not very precise. To the extent that order is not achieved exactly through scaling procedures, all subsequent empiricist procedures of association and relation will only compound the errors inherent in the scales. That scales are not measuring instruments means that their scope is limited to the population studied; therefore, any attempt to induce beyond the population studied to other populations at different times and places is impossible.

When empiricists are cognizant of these problems they usually call them "the measurement problem." The "measurement problem" is used, on the other hand, to explain the limits of systematic empiricism as a method. Systematic empiricism is supposed to be science, yet it results in no scientific laws (which every empiricist knows are generalizations with very high levels of relationship and very broad limits). Instead, the method results in very low levels of relationship and very limited scope. The fault must lie in the "measurement problem." Low levels of relatedness must be due to the fact that social scales only partly order data. Limited scope must be due to the limits of scope of existing measuring instruments. Weak empirical generalization must result from weak scales. "Good measurement" is, of course, difficult; measurement is always a problem or stumbling block in science; and when we are able to properly refine our scales, strong empirical generalizations with broad scope will follow. This, the final justification from an incredible disorganized mass of justifications, assumptions, and incantations, is pure bullshit. There is no reasoning behind it—just hot air.

The failure of systematic empiricism to produce exact science is inherent in the mistaken empirical observation that science is identical with empiricism. It is a result of empiricists evaluating science instead of scientists evaluating science. (No wonder that Bridgman could not understand Einstein's claim that theories are "free inventions.") Low levels of relatedness, limited scope, rigorous uncertainty of association, and so on are problems which follow from the assumption that the world is ordered (by God?) and that consequently there are (causal?) laws to be discovered by increasingly refined observational techniques. When scaling procedures are used in conjunction with systematic empiricism, there seems to be no limit to the number of hours which can be intensively spent in search of nothing. Belief in the measurement problem is an important ideological component of contemporary sociology in that it explains the lack of ability to discover laws. Apparently some practitioners feel that it is necessary to promote this belief, for if it were destroyed it would uncover the futility of the bulk of work in sociology.

Stevens and other operationalists believe that through refinement scaling procedures will result in more and more exactness and eventually in scientific metric measurement. This "idea" is supposedly made more plausible by calling metric measurement a "ratio scale" and ranking it on a level above the "interval scale" which itself ranks just above an "ordinal scale." But scaling procedures do not result in measurement and cannot be used to measure even in the sense that a yardstick can. "Scaling" is simply another word for averaging and composite ranking.

Scientific Measurement

While legitimating hours of fruitless labor in the social sciences, operationalism has also served to obscure the structure and logic of scientific measurement. Scientific measurement is not ratio scaling; in fact, it is not dependent on *any* empirical technique but is a consequence of a mathematically exact theory. To explain, predict, and manipulate the relations between observables, a scientific knowledge system uses concepts (nonobservables) theoretically related in theories and laws (mental inventions). If laws are to have any empirical use, they must be abstractively related to observables through their concepts. Abstractively relating a concept to particular empirical observations may be called an empirical interpretation of a concept. Measurement is a means by which a concept is empirically interpreted. Concepts are not observables and empirical measures thus cannot be definitions of concepts. The idea of operational definitions is contradictory to the meaning of concepts in science.

A concept directly connected with a measure for it is referred to as fundamental measurement. A concept which is fundamentally measured is often measured in more than one way depending on the empirical circumstances. In basic mechanics, for example, the concept of length may be measured by a yardstick, by laying standard rods end to end, by triangularization methods, calipers, rolling a wheel of known radius, and so forth. These are all legitimate procedures for measuring the concept of length as it occurs in Newtonian theory, because the results of each can enter isomorphically into the theory and form the basis of calculations. The result of the calculations must be isomorphic to the empirical circumstance to which it is applied, and this is the only empirical criterion of scientific measurement. The purpose of measurement is to order data so that the calculations of the theory are relevant to it.

On the other hand, none of the above methods of measuring length are satisfactory interpretations of the concept of length for certain interpretations of Einstein's theory of relativity.[9] A measurement is not and cannot be the definition of a concept (since concepts are nonobservational and are defined in terms of other concepts); and, therefore, the use of a multitude of measures (for length, for example) does not mean that a multitude of concepts have been generated. The choice of one measuring procedure over another is simply a result of empirical expediency according to the particular circumstances to which the law is being applied. There will be more than one fundamental measure developed for a concept when there are associated empirical circumstances in which the first either cannot be used at all, cannot be used accurately, or is particularly inconvenient to use. Since the scope of a concept does not refer to particular limited empirical circumstances and is empirically nonlimited, it is to be expected that one or another of three alternatives will eventually arise when a theory's application is extended.

The meaning of a measure and its type is a consequence of the

[9] See Albert Einstein, *The Meaning of Relativity* (Princeton, N.J.: Princeton University Press, 1955), pp. 3ff.

concept it refers to and the theory in which the concept occurs. The concepts which are measured are furthermore chosen as a consequence of the terms of the fundamental postulates of the theory, themselves abstractive statements. The first postulate of Newtonian mechanics, for example, refers to a continuing motion of a body in a straight line. A straight line implies the theoretical concept of length, continuation implies time, and body implies mass. Once these concepts are empirically interpreted, no more fundamental measurement is needed for that theory and related theories such as those of thermodynamics and electricity. The conception of length as a straight line (in the Euclidean sense) furthermore immediately implies that the measures for length mentioned above are appropriate, an implication which is fulfilled as those measures and the measures of the other concepts result (through calculation in the theoretical statement) in a value isomorphic to empirical observation. Thus it is clear that, if a theory and its postulates are understood, devising means for measuring its concepts is simply a matter of imaginative thinking in which the theory is related to observations by constructing some tool for ordering those observations. Even if the postulate were initially misinterpreted, this would soon be apparent from the lack of isomorphism between the laws and the conditions of their application. There is nothing mysterious about the meaning of measures in science; any procedure available for ordering observations in units (such as the ordering of an empirical interpretation of a length with a yardstick) may be legitimate. If we want to know then what the concept "length" means, the answer lies in the laws and postulates of the theory. The questions of what length "really is," what length is as an empirical reality, is meaningless in science. Length has a purely mental, theoretical meaning to the scientist, and to ask what it "really is" is to misunderstand the meaning of science. Length is not "what the yardstick measures" but instead the yardstick is a tool which allows empirical interpretations of the concept.

Scientific measurement is metric because the theories to which it is related are stated mathematically. If these measures did not have mathematical properties, they could not be used for interpretation of theories. On the other hand, without mathematical theories, scientific measurement is impossible. Measurement is measurement *of* something. In science it is measurement of empirical interpretations of concepts. Although measuring instruments such as the yardstick may have been used for practical empirical purposes many centuries before the development of scientific laws, the mere existence of those measures did not lead to those laws. Operationalist procedures, no matter how refined and cultivated, cannot lead to scientific measurement.

Most scientific concepts are not measured fundamentally but by derivation from fundamentals through the relationships of laws. In derived measurement a concept is empirically interpreted through its relationship in the theory to other terms which are fundamentally measured. For example, a simple balance scale provides a derived measure for mass (or weight) using one of the laws of levers. This law states that mass times length on one side of a fulcrum is equal to mass times length on the other ($ML = M^1L^1$), and "equal" is empirically interpreted as being in balance. Two types of scales can be devised, one in which L is varied by moving a standard mass along one lever arm to balance an unknown mass at a known length on the other, or one in which M is varied as in a simple pan balance with fixed lengths of levers and the masses on both sides varied. (On the other hand, the common bathroom scale uses a spring and may be interpreted according to Hooke's law, $F = KX^2$.) Mass, however, can be fundamentally measured by alternating weights between two pans on a balance with lever arms of undetermined length until two weights were found which balanced perfectly in either pan. These would be used similarly to generate more weights, and through the law of levers ($ML = M^1L^1$) one could determine that the lengths are equal and thus derive a measure of length from a fundamental measure of mass. Thus it does not matter which concepts are fundamentally measured and which are measured by derivation as long as the theory is capable of generating one from the other through theoretic connection or abstractive connection to observables.

Concepts measured fundamentally and those measured by derivation should not be (and are not) treated differently in theoretical calculations. Most concepts are never fundamentally measured (concepts such as velocity, magnetism, force, heat, and temperature); but, because they occur in a theoretical network, derived measures may be calculated in various ways. Velocity (or at least average speed) can be derived from time and length. Instantaneous speed can be read from an automobile speedometer (a simple generator in which output force is balanced by a spring) through derivations from electromagnetic theory and Hooke's law.

In the application of a theory to a broad range of phenomena, the opportunities to derive measures in different directions through various means is often crucial to being able to measure at all. For everyday purposes we measure temperature with a simple mercury thermometer in which the measure of the concept of temperature is derived through the ideal gas law, $\frac{PV}{T} = K$. But one cannot plunge a conventional thermometer into an object cold enough to approach absolute zero (a theoretical quantity) and expect to get a meaningful reading. As a consequence of the theory of thermodynamics, however, we may conclude that very cold objects have little resistance to electrical current and that this resistance approaches zero as the temperature of absolute zero is approached. As a consequence, the temperature of very cold objects may be measured by measuring resistance to an electrical current and calculating back to the temperature. A temperature value is thus calculated as a consequence of a theory.

It is thus preposterous from the point of view of science to think of temperature as a quality of an object to be discovered by improving empirical scaling techniques, even though operationalists such as Stevens assume that "temperature became an interval scale with the development of thermometry and, after thermodynamics had used the expansion ratio of gases to extrapolate to zero, it became a ratio scale."[10] Such confusion is a result of the backward idea that the statement affirms the consequent. Stevens discusses absolute zero as if it were an observable point on a measuring scale, which indeed it would *have to be* from his perspective. But there is no absolute zero in nature (what has to be is not), so it cannot have been discovered empirically by operations. Absolute zero is a theoretical entity having no empirical existence. If Stevens were right, then such an event as the "discovery" of the yardstick would

[10] S. S. Stevens, "Measurement, Psychophysics and Utility," in *Measurement: Definitions and Theories* (New York: John Wiley & Sons, 1959), pp. 24–25.

mean that the development of a ratio scale (the level of scientific measurement) for length had been discovered (apparently as a refinement of an interval scale of length)—an obvious absurdity. Following the theory, the zero point of length can represent any empirical place. Without the theory, how can the empiricist–operationalist find the "natural origin" for length if an infinite number of possible zero points exist? Even an expedition to scout the globe with a large number of well-trained observers (having excellent observational techniques and a knowledge of the best operational scaling techniques) is doomed to expensive failure. (Maybe the "natural origin" is on Mars?)

According to Stevens, "measurement is the business of pinning numbers on things." [11] This is, indeed, the practice operationalists follow, and they fortunately seem not to have reached a limit to their supply of pins, although eventually they may do so, if only because there seem to be so many different "things." The practice of "assigning numerals to objects or events according to rule—any rule" [12] (unguided by theory) can result only in observational categories in isolation from one another. All kinds of statistical associations can be made, but they have no theoretical import. In fact, if objects are not interpreted according to a theory which dictates a relationship, one can just as meaningfully make arbitrary statistical associations between the "status" of people and the number of fleas on a cow as between "status" and "family background." The former has just as much scientific meaning.

Since, to the operationalist, the outcome of the scaling operation defines the term, then two different measures represent two different concepts unless they are found to be "approximately equal" in enough empirical cases to allow generalization.[13] It is rather strange that they (as empiricists) failed to discover that the history of science has recorded no case in which a concept has been split because there was more than one measure for it (although there are many perfectly solid concepts with more than one measure).

Operationalism (or empiricism) and science represent two completely different knowledge systems. The meaning of terms such

[11] *Ibid.*, p. 18.

[12] *Ibid.*, p. 19.

[13] See Dingle, "A Theory of Measurements," p. 7.

as *concepts, theories,* and *laws* is so different that there is no possibility that development of the former could ever turn it into the latter. From the point of view of science it makes no sense to attempt to establish exact measurement unless one has a theory. Operationalism is an empiricist attempt to understand scientific measurement. If the understanding of measurement by operationalists can be used as an operational measure of the ability of operationalism to understand, then it is a failure. Operationalism is a nonrational interpretation of scientific measurement which is superficially plausible only to an empiricist.

At the beginning of his research, the empiricist is confronted by a universe of incredible complexity. How can he properly observe it? Operationalism simplifies this problem for him: just set down some rules and see what you want to see. From this we get scaling procedures and then "quantification." Later, when our scales are perfected (by solving the "measurement problem") and all the facts are in, we will have scientific sociology.

Scaling begins with the assumption that the world is ordered. Thus scales are constructed to be ordered by data. Measurement begins with the scientific concern of imposing an understood order on observable phenomena. Measures, therefore, order data. It follows from this distinction that scaling and measurement are completely unrelated pursuits.

8 *the philosophy of empirical science*

Empirical social science has often followed the methods and ideas of philosophers of science, particularly those of the "logical empiricists" or "logical positivists." This philosophical school (like many others) is concerned with the search for the "truth." In this search for truth they begin with the assumption that the truth is knowable through the proper "scientific" techniques of investigation including (1) accurate measuring instruments, (2) objectivity of observation, and (3) induction from the resulting accurate observations to "general empirical laws." The logical empiricists, however, differ from the pure empiricists in that they believe that these general laws must be stated formally using "pure logic" and that particular empirical cases are explained by deduction from them. From this point of view science consists of a set of induced general laws about observable phenomena which, coupled with a set of particular observations of phenomena, allow us to deductively predict or explain associated empirical phenomena.[1]

[1] See Karl R. Popper, *The Logic of Scientific Discovery* (London: Hutchinson, 1959), p. 32.

Bertrand Russell pointed out that it is clear, following David Hume's argument, that cause–effect explanations are based on past and present observations and cannot be projected to the future with certainty. Pure empiricism cannot generate universal scientific laws. He notes, on the other hand, that science is characterized by universality or determinative relations and he attributes this deterministic character to the use of pure logic. In pure logic there is a determinativeness that is a consequence of its formal structure. Thus, if logic begins with general true statements, the conclusions arrived at when they are combined with accurate particular statements must necessarily be true simply because of their form.

But here the logical empiricists have solved their problem mainly by ignoring its existence. Pure logic indeed arrives at determinative conclusions, but the problem still stands—where do general laws come from? Their answer, of course, is again couched in the terms of logic. According to Hans Reichenbach, it is inductive logic which yields general laws. But this is no solution at all; it merely assigns a label to empirical generalization, hiding its tentative, nondeterminative character by calling it "logic." Inductive reasoning proceeds from particular observations to a general statement of association which still ties us to the past and present and does not allow us to project its relevance to the future. Although the particular statements upon which it is based may very well be "true," we cannot know the general statement is true. If our general statement is not necessarily true, neither are the conclusions we can draw from its use. Thus "pure logic" cannot draw necessary conclusions by deduction from inductive general statements. The only general statements which can lead to true necessary conclusions in pure logic are those which are "true" by definition, and these are nonpredictive. If it is true by definition that all swans are white we simply do not admit the existence of black swans but call those birds which look like swans but are black by some other name ("snaws"). We cannot predict that if we find a swan he will be white but we will call "swans" only birds which we observe to be white.

Karl Popper, indeed, denies the possibility of the use of induction to arrive at general laws. In fact, he even denies that inductive inferences may be "probable" or specified in terms of probability.

Clearly the universality of a general law cannot be a matter of "degree" or the law would not be universal. The attempt to introduce probability in induction of general laws says essentially that sometimes the law is true and sometimes it is not. Obviously this sort of law is neither universal nor useful for predictive purposes. Popper states that there is no general logic by which we can construct scientific laws but that they are instead the result of a "creative intuition." But if general empirical laws are arrived at through some mental operation on observations, "creative intuition" can only be another label for generalizing from particular observations.

Nevertheless, although Popper does not believe that laws result from any empirical–logical procedure and are not the product of induction from observed true particulars, they are empirical laws which are subject to empirical test. These empirical laws are submitted to empirical test in "practical applications and experiments"; they are *falsified* if our tests do not agree with them. The method of testing is "deductive." [2] Popper views scientific explanation as *causal* explanation in which the "*explanation* of an event means to deduce a statement which describes it, using as premises of the deduction one or more *universal laws,* together with certain singular statements, the *initial conditions.*" [3] Scientific laws, then, are empirical–causal statements descriptive of real connections between events and are empirically true or false. If they can be empirically true or false then their truth or falsity is determined by observation. At best this means that a law may have been true for the past and is only a hypothetical description of possible future events. If it is only hypothetical for the future it cannot form a basis for prediction since the next observation may "falsify" it.

Popper's empirical–causal law is simply a hypothetical general statement. Any relational statement capable of falsification cannot be a scientific law since it clearly is not universal in its scope of application. We find in actual use of law, however, that they are not falsifiable but that contrary observations led to the revision of laws to broaden their scope, the refinement of our measurements, or to other maneuvers designed to retain the laws in spite of our

[2] See *ibid.,* p. 33.

[3] *Ibid.,* p. 59.

observations. A law is rejected only if another one better explains the observed facts, not because it has been found to be false. The assumption made by Popper and others is that laws describe reality in which case they must be either true or false, but if laws are rationalistic in form they do not describe reality but order observation and are discarded only if they fail to order it adequately.

Scientific laws are not "true" or "false," and neither are they verified "deductively." If an experiment were run in nuclear physics in which the mass–energy of a system was measured at two times and was found to be less at time two than time one, Popper would have us believe that the law of conservation of mass–energy was falsified and that the physicist would rush to publish his amazing results. But on the contrary, the physicist is more certain of his law than of any single set of observations and measurements. If the measurements were properly carried out, the discrepancy may be attributed to the inadequacy of the measuring instrument used (something simply was not measured) but the law is not disbelieved. Considering the type of measurements done and the law, it is possible to calculate that the measurements as originally carried out failed to measure something; and, from that conclusion, new measuring instruments can be constructed to include a measure of the quantity missed the first time. The result of experiments inconsistent with the law would not be (as Popper would have us believe) the immediate rejection of the law, but may, on the contrary, lead to the postulation of a new particle hitherto unmeasured. In this case instead of falsifying the law by empirical evidence, we may arrive at new observations by accepting the law as unfalsifiable.

Although new laws of broader scope may be devised when experimental results inconsistent with the original law are repeatedly found, a law is never rejected by the results of a single experiment. Laws are theoretic statements relating nonobservable concepts, and experiments are concerned with observables; consequently a single experiment giving results inconsistent with a law does not falsify the law. On the other hand, a single experiment might determine the acceptance of one law over another, but neither law would be regarded as false. Bridges built according to Newtonian theory are not built on false knowledge. Falsification is not a component of scientific practice.

Carl Hempel systematized the logical empiricists' idea of deductive explanation in science in his paper "The Function of General Laws in History." It comes as no surprise that Hempel cites no general laws in that paper and shows no application to history; but at the same time he refers to a "metaphysical theory of history," apparently intending this label to apply to Karl Marx. From an empiricist view of science Marx may very well have presented a "metaphysical theory," but from the viewpoint of scientific knowledge systems this intended negative criticism is actually a compliment to Marx, who (unlike those who search for empirical "patterns" in history) based his view of history on theoretic relations of concepts. Hempel himself confused systematic empiricism with science.

According to Hempel, a "deductive nomological" explanation involves the use of a set of general laws L_1, L_2, L_3, . . . , L_n, a set of statements of observed events, C_1, C_2, C_3, . . . , C_n, and *E*, a sentence containing the predicted or explained event which is arrived at deductively from the premises (*L*s and *C*s). Prediction and explanation are thus both consequences of the use of deductive logic, going from premises including empirical generalizations and particular observations to a conclusion involving an event to be explained or predicted. But, if a general law (*L*) is simply a generalization (or an induction from previous observations), any additional *C*s simply add to the law itself and cannot be used deductively to predict or explain *E*, which itself can be no more than a test of the truth or falsity of the general law. A general law, *L*, if it is indeed a consequence of generalization, is less sure than particular observations, *C*s, on which it is based; consequently, even if we could explain *E*s by deduction, our explanation would be less sure than the observations on which it was based. Although Hempel claimed he was speaking of the process of explanation and Karl Popper claimed he was dealing only with the process of verification of scientific laws, both were indeed speaking of the same logical deductive problem of relating an individual event *E* to a general empirical statement *L* in which *E* may itself be true, may be directly observed to be true or false, but where *L* is uncertain. If true general statements can only be true by definition, then general laws based on observations cannot be necessarily true, and predictions and explanations are always unsure. If the prediction does not hold up, the law is falsified.

If laws are based on empirical generalization they contain no more than the observations themselves, and explanation is reduced to nothing more than a statement of what is or more accurately, what was. These explanations are causal explanations of the form *A* has been observed with *B*, and *B* is said to be explained by the observation of *A*. If *B* does not occur when *A* occurs, the law is falsified. If *A* occurs and *B* does not, the law is falsified. We cannot predict from a causal explanation which is based on an assumption of causal connection. The causal connection itself cannot be observed, so our observation is incomplete, and the connection is tentative. Nothing is predicted or explained if the event itself is more certain than the law supposedly explaining it. The event is a test of the statement, not a prediction from it.

The statement, "All *A*s are *B*s," if it is not a definition but an empirical generalization, really means no more than "*A*s have been observed with *B*s." But this statement is not a universal statement, but limited to a population. As such, it cannot form a major premise in a deductive explanation. Consequently no empirical generalization can act as a major premise in a deductive explanation, and *empirical generalizations can never be used deductively to explain or predict.*

Statistical explanation which Hempel includes as a type of scientific explanation involves the application of "probabilistic" relational statements to particular events. The structure of statistical explanation is analogous to deductive explanation (although Hempel calls it "inductive") in that a general relational statement and a specific factual statement are used to derive a conclusion about a specific fact. For example, an explanation of John Jones's recovery from a streptococcus infection would involve the following:

Premise *A*: The probability of recovery from a streptococcus infection when treated by penicillin is close to 1.

Premise *B*: John Jones was treated with large doses of penicillin.

Conclusion: The probability that John Jones will recover from his streptococcus infection is close to 1.

Hempel calls probability statements such as Premise *A* "statistical laws." It is apparent that these "laws" suffer from the same logical problems and problems of application as the other "general laws" he described. Predictions and explanations cannot be made from them. John Jones either does or does not recover. If he does recover the probability value of statement *A* is slightly increased by his case, and if he does not the probability value decreases. Not only is the statistical relationship as unsure as a causal relationship, its value varies with the event it is supposed to predict and is altered by it, while the event itself cannot be predicted with any certainty. Furthermore, if John Jones either recovers or does not, he does not recover with a probability of close to 1. Statistical explanations based on sociological findings are of this sort, except that our "probability" values are usually much lower. The doctor may use penicillin on John Jones with some hope for his recovery since it has been used many times with great success, but we have no such confidence in our sociological statistical findings. Knowledge of empirical association is often useful in practical situations, but it explains nothing. John Jones may indeed have recovered because he was given penicillin, but this *explains* nothing. Our knowledge consists of no more than the knowledge that (*A*) a great many people who have had penicillin have recovered from streptococcus infections, (*B*) John Jones was given penicillin, and (*C*) John Jones recovered (or did not recover) from his streptococcus infection. This explanation is not "inductive" as Hempel calls it because it involves no general statement, and it is not even deductive, for it has no major premise.

Scientific explanation cannot be deductive because scientific laws are statements relating nonobservable concepts, such as force, mass, and acceleration in terms of nonobservable connectives such as an equivalence or an equals sign. If our major premise consisted of $f = ma$ where f, m, and a are defined by their relationship to each other and not by observables, we could not set up a deductive explanation at all, for it would take the following form:

Minor premise *A*: $f = ma$, where the terms are nonobservable.

Major premise *B*: A value of *X* for *F* in terms of an observational definition of force.

Major premise *C*: A value of *X* for *M* in terms of an observational definition of mass.

Conclusion *D*: A value for *A*, which is illegitimately deduced because the *f* and *m* in the minor premise are not the same as the *F* and *M* in the major premises.

If the terms and relations of a scientific law are nonobservables, explanation cannot be made deductively with minor premises consisting of observable terms and relations. Since it is not possible to combine laws with observationals in deductive explanation, laws cannot be falsified through observation. Laws are instead applied by relating them abstractively to observations. In scientific explanation, particular observations are abstractively related to the law, calculations are carried out with the quantity so derived plugged into the law itself, and the result is abstractively interpreted back to other observations.

Empirical philosophy turns science into "empirical science," confuses abstraction with generalization and concepts with observational categories. Those who attempt to construct science in accordance with such thinking will end up with empiricism instead.

from empiricism to scientific sociology

9 Sociological "findings" are not general knowledge. They thus are useless either as empiricist or scientific knowledge because they have no application. A statement of general empirical knowledge, an empirical generalization, is based on the observation of similarities (either objects or events) and consists of a classification of those similarities according to the criteria by which they are said to be similar. This knowledge is used in practical daily activities because of the expectation that these similarities will continue to be observed. Sociological findings, however, are not general because they deal with averages, summaries, or proportions which are descriptive of particular groups or populations. In fact, no matter how many individuals are included in the finding, the result is always a descriptive particular. On the other hand, an average does not reflect similarities but summarizes a range of differences. Sociological findings are not general knowledge—they are instead particularistic descriptions which say nothing about other particulars. Findings are, at best, useless, particularistic empirical knowledge.

In the attempt to accurately portray observations, the systematic empiricist mistakes the "general" quality of generalization which is achieved by sorting and classifying for generality achieved by including as many empirical cases as possible. The former proceeds by eliminating as many particularistic differences as possible, the latter by including as many as possible. But including "all the facts" means that empirical generalization will never be achieved, and any averaging or summarizing description of the results of such a procedure is necessarily a particular, for the facts simply cannot be accurately reported as a generalization. The statement that "a cow has four legs" is not the result of averaging at all but comes from deliberately ignoring those "cows" which do not. We might find that the average "cow" (if we could decide what a cow is without ignoring some particulars) has 3.991 legs, but in that case we would be unable to apply our finding because we would find few particular animals with that many legs.

Besides, at least six additional characteristics of the findings of systematic empiricism make them impossible to use in the explanation of social events. These were each discussed in earlier chapters. Each of these conditions is inherent in the method itself, and each one taken independently is a sufficient reason why explanation is impossible.

1. Even if the particularistic findings that result from the method were empirical generalizations, they would be incapable of either explanation or prediction. Since generalizations are themselves no more than statements based on the observation of a set of particulars from the past, they cannot be said to include information about the future (are not universal); therefore they cannot be used to either explain or predict individual events. A generalization does not explain the particulars which make it up because it is defined by them and does not explain or predict other particulars because those particulars are not included in the scope of the generalization and might indeed contradict it. Although a generalization may be used by individuals in their mundane affairs (for example, John Doe may use one to decide how many martinis he may have without acting like a fool), it does not have the power of explanation offered by science. Furthermore, so-called deductive systems of explanation can not be properly constructed because the empirical generalization which empiricists would use for the major premise is not

in fact a logical universal and consequently cannot be used with a factual specification in a deductive explanation.

2. The test of association used by the systematic empiricists entails a logical fallacy and produces "rigorous uncertainty." But individual facts either occur or they do not. Certain facts cannot be explained by uncertain statements. Even in ordinary everyday practical empiricism we do not make that error.

3. The terms of findings of systematic empiricism are not related absolutely but by "empirical probability," according to indexes such as correlation. Although the possible variance of the correlation value is from zero to an absolute value of one (a perfect correlation), Pearson and other empiricists claim that the value of one is never reached but only approached. It is obvious that a relational statement concerned only with indeterminate relations between terms cannot be used to *derive* results and consequently is of no use in the explanation of events.

4. The procedures of induction practiced by the proponents of systematic empiricism are concerned with induction to a transitory collectivity (from a sample to a population) whose permanence they are powerless to control. Although a set of "findings" may have been descriptively accurate for a population at the time and place of the study, they are not necessarily relevant even to other similar groups at the time of their publication. They are, in fact, of no utility in application to any population (but the original) regardless of time and place. Inductive procedures may indeed produce descriptive knowledge about the past, but they are of no use for present explanation or future predictions.

5. Operationalist scaling procedures are methods of approximate (average or composite) post-factum descriptive ranking. They are not measurement procedures and may not be used to measure any new circumstances whatsoever. The terms of these descriptive rankings cannot be interpreted for cases outside the sample studied and thus are devoid of meaning for use in the explanation of new cases.

6. In actual practice, the sociological experiment and survey do not satisfactorily generate empirical generalizations even according to the criteria of association, relationship, and induction of the systematic empiricism. Empiricist induction is based on likeness, but lab experiments are by definition unlike natural cases and thus

any inductions from them for application in social circumstances are illegitimate. The survey, on the other hand, cannot utilize empirically meaningful controls, and thus cannot result in associations with more assurance than arbitrary guessing. Only the field experiment is logically capable of generating results satisfying the systematic empiricists' criteria and then only if the empirical power of the researcher is strong enough to effectively (or absolutely) control the empirical circumstances. But until sociologists become philosopher kings or are delegated total power over the environment of their experiments by a totalitarian government, the field experiment is as useless as the others.

Sociological research methods are not good empirical methods because they do not result in empirical generalizations, and they are not scientific methods at all. Their outcome, the finding, has, in fact, no phenomenological status whatsoever. Sociological findings fail to meet the criteria of knowledge by any standards and fail so miserably that the authorities who maintain them have found it necessary to cover up their lack of meaning under a blanket of legitimizations. Beyond the many legitimizations already discussed in the previous chapters, there is the "philosophical argument" that social events by their very nature (inherently different from physical events) cannot be exactly explained and predicted. Social events are said to be too complex, and occasionally the issue of free will is brought in as if it were some sort of sociological uncertainty principle. Such claims are merely justifications for the failure of empiricist methods to produce science. Certainly social facts are unbelievably complex if we have no theories to understand them; but physical facts do not differ in that respect. Likewise, our values are tied in with both social and physical observations; objectivity in reporting the facts is thus a basic problem with knowledge based only on observation—empiricism. The claim that man's "free will" messes up prediction in social science involves both a colossal egotism which assumes that man's will is somehow independent of his existence and an empiricist concentration on individuals which precludes the development of general knowledge. Given the assumptions of empiricism, scientific knowledge can never be obtained. The knowledge obtained in any field cannot be independent of its methods. The empiricist procedures of sociology could not result in knowledge useful for explanation, regardless of the area in which they were used. The lack of predictive and explanatory power in sociology can therefore be explained as a simple consequence of the methods used, and it is not necessary to make any assumptions about the special nature of social phenomena. What such claims amount to, in fact, is that we do not wish to take the responsibility for our own failure and are trying to hide it by blaming it on the phenomena.

When its application is limited to simple actions, empiricism has practical value. Trial and error learning and routinization of action through practice may provide adequate means for building houses, driving cars, or fishing. But John Stuart Mill confused such simple practical knowledge with science, and his confusions were confounded by the statisticians, resulting in the battered facts or "findings" of systematic empiricism. Systematic empiricism, although it is terribly complex, provides "knowledge" of no practical utility. Instead of rejecting their methods in order to build science, the sociological empiricists have followed their assumptions to the methodological dead end inherent within them.

Empiricism, when it works, works only with observations of what is and what was. It concludes (since observation is the criterion of knowledge) that what is, is and must be. In the social realm this means that empiricism is inherently conservative. Since its procedures of generating new combinations are through the power of control, its necessary social outcome is totalitarianism.

Science, however, ignores what is and what was, often denying observation in order to generate theoretical postulates. Empiricism is inherently unimaginative and conservative. Science is inherently imaginative and radical. Science assumes no empirical truths and thus is not restricted by them. But "radical sociologists" trained in unimaginative empiricism confuse the totalitarian tendencies of systematic empiricism with science and thereby render themselves and their actions impotent.

Sociological knowledge is not scientific, but it could be. The methods of achieving scientific sociology, however, can not include either new statistical procedures or scaling methods. Empiricism is not science, and systematic empiricism is not even good empiricism. A scientific sociology implies a completely different method.

index